THE
CHARGE
OF THE
LIGHT
BRIGADE

AND OTHER STORY POEMS

Edited by Marjorie L. Burns
Design by Marijka Kostiw

Cover Handtint by Bill Kobasz / Reliable Design Studios
On our cover, Captain Geoffrey Vickers (Errol Flynn) leads the Charge of the Light Brigade in a scene from the 1936 Warner Brothers film based on the poem by Alfred, Lord Tennyson.

ISBN 0-590-35585-6

12 11 10 9 8 7 6 5 4   3/9
                                                                          31

ACKNOWLEDGMENTS

Grateful acknowledgment is made to the following authors and publishers for the use of copyrighted materials. Every effort has been made to obtain permission to use previously published material. Any errors or omissions are unintentional.

BMG Music for "Ode to Billy Joe" by Bobbie Gentry, © 1967 Northridge Music Company. Used by permission. All rights reserved.

Curtis Brown, Ltd. for "The Adventures of Isabel" by Ogden Nash. Reprinted by permission of Curtis Brown, Ltd. Copyright © 1945 by Ogden Nash.

George Duckworth & Co. Ltd. for Canadian rights to "Matilda" from CAUTION-ARY VERSES by Hilaire Belloc. By permission of Duckworth.

Feinman and Krasilovsky, Attorneys, for "The Cremation of Sam McGee" by Robert W. Service from SONGS OF A SOURDOUGH. Reprinted by permission of William Krasilovsky.

Hugh Noyes for "The Highwayman" by Alfred A. Noyes. From COLLECTED POEMS by Alfred Noyes. Copyright 1906, 1934 by Alfred Noyes. Reprinted by permission of Hugh Noyes.

Putnam Publishing Group for "The Cremation of Sam McGee" by Robert W. Service. Reprinted by permission of The Putnam Publishing Group from SONGS OF A SOURDOUGH by Robert Service. Copyright © 1916 by G.P. Putnam's Sons.

Random House, Inc. for "Matilda" from CAUTIONARY VERSES by Hilaire Belloc. Published 1941 by Alfred A. Knopf, Inc. For "Dunkirk" from DUNKIRK by Robert Nathan. Copyright © 1941 and renewed 1969 by Robert Nathan. Reprinted by permission of Alfred A. Knopf, Inc.

Norma Untermeyer for "The Erl-King" by Johann Wolfgang von Goethe, translated by Louis Untermeyer. For "The Frogs Who Wanted a King" by Joseph Lauren. Reprinted by permission of Norma Untermeyer.

Viking Penguin, Inc. for "Biographies," from ENOUGH ROPE by Dorothy Parker. Copyright 1926, renewed 1954 by Dorothy Parker. All rights reserved. Reprinted by permission of Viking Penguin, a division of Penguin Books USA, Inc.

CONTENTS

GROUP 3 HEROES AND VILLAINS

GROUP 4 BALLADS OLD AND NEW

GROUP 5 LOVE AND LOYALTY

INTRODUCTION

What form of entertainment is thousands of years old and still popular in every corner of the world? It is the narrative poem — the poem that tells a story. Its characters may be kings and queens or ordinary men and women, rich or poor, brave or cowardly, heroes or villains. The story may be sad or silly, true or fictional, inspiring or frightening. But, always, the story poem combines the power of poetical language (rhythm, rhyme, vivid imagery) with the excitement of a rattling good tale.

Narrative poems have been around at least since the time of the ancient Greeks, and probably even longer. Originally they were either recited from memory or set to music and sung. Even today in some parts of the world, epics — long poems celebrating the deeds of real or legendary heroes and heroines — are still recited or sung at public gatherings. One performer may recite for three hours without a break, while the audience listens entranced, even though the tale may be old and familiar.

In this book you will find narrative poems on a wide variety of topics. You will read about a Revolutionary War patriot (Paul Revere in "Paul Revere's Ride"), a famous battle ("The Charge of the Light Brigade"), an eerie encounter with a goblin ("The Erl-King"), and the desperate sacrifice of a girl who loved an outlaw ("The Highwayman"). But as you read, remember that, by tradition, narrative poems are meant for the ear, not the eye. So, while you scan the printed words, try to hear them in your mind. Better yet, get together with friends and take turns reading or reciting the poems out loud. That way, you will enjoy them more, and you will understand more clearly why this ancient form of entertainment is still so widely enjoyed.

GROUP 1

PATRIOTISM

AND

ADVENTURE

The event described in this poem took place on October 25, 1854, during a battle between Russian and British troops in the Crimean War. Russian foot soldiers and artillery held one end of a valley and the hills on both sides of it. Because of confusion in the relaying of a message, the light-armored brigade of cavalry under Lord Cardigan was ordered to charge the length of the valley and attack the cannons at the end. Of the 670 men who began the charge, almost 300 were killed. The battle itself was unimportant and has been largely forgotten. But, thanks to Tennyson's poem, the charge of the Light Brigade has become a symbol for magnificent courage in the face of hopeless odds.

THE CHARGE OF THE LIGHT BRIGADE

Half a league, half a league,
  Half a league onward,
All in the valley of Death
  Rode the six hundred.
"Forward, the Light Brigade!
Charge for the guns!" he said:
Into the valley of Death
  Rode the six hundred.

"Forward, the Light Brigade!"
Was there a man dismay'd?
Not tho' the soldier knew
  Someone had blunder'd:
Theirs not to make reply,
Theirs not to reason why,
Theirs but to do and die:
Into the valley of Death
  Rode the six hundred.

Cannon to right of them,
Cannon to left of them,
Cannon in front of them
　　Volley'd and thunder'd;
Storm'd at with shot and shell,
Boldly they rode and well,
Into the jaws of Death,
Into the mouth of Hell
　　Rode the six hundred.

Flash'd all their sabres bare,
Flash'd as they turn'd in air,
Sabring the gunners there,
Charging an army, while
　　All the world wonder'd:
Plunged in the battery-smoke
Right thro' the line they broke;
Cossack and Russian
Reel'd from the sabre-stroke
　　Shatter'd and sunder'd.
Then they rode back, but not,
　　Not the six hundred.

Cannon to right of them,
Cannon to left of them,
Cannon behind them
　　Volley'd and thunder'd;
Stormed at with shot and shell,
While horse and hero fell,
They that had fought so well
Came thro' the jaws of Death,
Back from the mouth of Hell,
All that was left of them,
　　Left of six hundred.

When can their glory fade?
O the wild charge they made!
 All the world wonder'd.
Honour the charge they made!
Honour the Light Brigade,
 Noble six hundred.

ALFRED, LORD TENNYSON

PAUL REVERE'S RIDE

Listen, my children, and you shall hear
Of the midnight ride of Paul Revere,
On the eighteenth of April, in Seventy-five;
Hardly a man is now alive
Who remembers that famous day and year.

He said to his friend, "If the British march
By land or sea from the town tonight,
Hang a lantern aloft in the belfry arch
Of the North Church tower as a signal light —
One, if by land, and two, if by sea;
And I on the opposite shore will be,
Ready to ride and spread the alarm
Through every Middlesex village and farm,
For the country folk to be up and to arm."
Then he said "Good-night," and with muffled oar
Silently row'd to the Charlestown shore,
Just as the moon rose over the bay,
Where swinging wide at her moorings lay
The *Somerset*, British man-of-war;
A phantom ship, with each mast and spar
Across the moon like a prison bar,
And a huge black hulk, that was magnified
By its own reflection in the tide.

Meanwhile his friend, through alley and street,
Wanders and watches with eager ears,
Till in the silence around him he hears
The master of men at the barrack-door,
The sound of arms, and the tramp of feet,
And the measured tread of the grenadiers
Marching down to their boats on the shore.

Then he climb'd the tower of the Old North Church,
By the wooden stairs, with stealthy tread,
To the belfry-chamber overhead,
And startled the pigeons from their perch
On the sombre rafters, that round him made
Masses of moving shapes of shade —
By the trembling ladder, steep and tall,
To the highest window in the wall,
Where he paused to listen and look down
A moment on the roofs of the town,
And the moonlight flowing over all.

Beneath, in the churchyard, lay the dead,
In their night-encampment on the hill,
Wrapp'd in silence so deep and still
That he could hear, like a sentinel's tread,
The watchful night-wind, as it went
Creeping along from tent to tent,
And seeming to whisper, "All is well!"
A moment only he feels the spell
Of the place and the hour, and the secret dread
Of the lonely belfry and the dead;
For suddenly all his thoughts are bent
On a shadowy something far away,
Where the river widens to meet the bay,
A line of black that bends and floats
On the rising tide like a bridge of boats.

Meanwhile, impatient to mount and ride,
Booted and spurr'd, with a heavy stride
On the opposite shore walk'd Paul Revere.
Now he patted his horse's side,
Now he gazed at the landscape far and near,
Then, impetuous, stamp'd the earth,

And turn'd and tighten'd his saddle-girth;
But mostly he watch'd with eager search
The belfry-tower of the Old North Church,
As it rose above the graves on the hill,
Lonely and spectral and sombre and still.
And lo! as he looks, on the belfry's height
A glimmer, and then a gleam of light!
He springs to the saddle, the bridle he turns,
But lingers and gazes, till full on his sight
A second lamp in the belfry burns.

A hurry of hoofs in a village street,
A shape in the moonlight, a bulk in the dark,
And beneath, from the pebbles, in passing, a spark
Struck out by a steed flying fearless and fleet:
That was all; and yet, through the gloom and the light,
The fate of a nation was riding that night;
And the spark struck out by that steed in his flight
Kindled the land into flame with its heat.

He had left the village and mounted the steep,
And beneath him, tranquil and broad and deep,
Is the Mystic, meeting the ocean tides,
And under the alders that skirt its edge,
Now soft on the sand, now loud on the ledge,
Is heard the tramp of his steed as he rides.

It was twelve by the village clock
When he crossed the bridge into Medford town.
He heard the crowing of the cock,
And the barking of the farmer's dog,
And felt the damp of the river fog,
That rises after the sun goes down.

It was one by the village clock
When he galloped into Lexington.
He saw the gilded weathercock
Swim in the moonlight as he pass'd,
And the meeting-house windows, blank and bare,
Gaze at him with a spectral glare,
As if they already stood aghast
At the bloody work they would look upon.

It was two by the village clock
When he came to the bridge in Concord town.
He heard the bleating of the flock,
And the twitter of birds among the trees,
And felt the breath of the morning breeze
Blowing over the meadows brown.
And one was safe and asleep in his bed
Who at the bridge would be first to fall,
Who that day would be lying dead,
Pierced by a British musket-ball.

You know the rest; in the books you have read,
How the British regulars fired and fled,
How the farmers gave them ball for ball,
From behind each fence and farmyard wall,
Chasing the red-coats down the lane,
Then crossing the fields to emerge again
Under the trees at the turn of the road,
And only pausing to fire and load.

So through the night rode Paul Revere,
And so through the night went his cry of alarm
To every Middlesex village and farm —
A cry of defiance, and not of fear,
A voice in the darkness, a knock at the door,
And a word that shall echo for evermore!

For, borne on the night-wind of the Past,
Through all our history, to the last,
In the hour of darkness, and peril, and need,
The people will waken and listen to hear
The hurrying hoof-beats of that steed,
And the midnight message of Paul Revere.

HENRY WADSWORTH LONGFELLOW

When Paul Revere rode through Lexington and Concord on April 18,
1775, to warn of the approach of British troops, farmers and villagers took
up arms to defend their right to independence. But some who took part in
the opening skirmishes of the Revolutionary War were hardly old enough
to understand why they were there.

EPITAPH FOR A CONCORD BOY

Now there is none of the living who can remember
How quietly the sun came into the village of Concord,
No one who will know of the sun in the eyes of the dead
    boy
There on the village green, where he fell.

He did not fall because he hated the Redcoats,
Indeed, he would have known little of them
Had not that quick, grim man, his father,
Hurried him dutifully toward the crackle of musketry.

His father had routed him out and stuck a gun in his hand
And then said something about the "country's
    deliverance,"
Until the boy went, rubbing the dreams from his eyes
And stood on the green with the others, facing the
    soldiers.

When the Redcoat leader had shouted, "Disperse, ye
    rebels,"
The boy would have gone back to his bed willingly,
But as no one else went, he stayed, watching the elegant
    enemy.
He was never aware the volley of war had been sounded.

Shot through the heart he took less time to die
Than the rabbits he had himself killed, many a day.

Though when his tight hand clutched at his own blood
It was as if he had never met death, entirely.

Once, for a split second, he wondered
Why he could not raise his strong legs from the grass,
And why the slow granite of his father's face
Was melting above him, for it never had.

He would have spoken now to his father, but the words
　　were not there.
Plainly the thoughts for his tongue were bound in his plow-
　　taut hands,
In the fields out of Concord he had said what he could with
　　them,
And now when his heart grew dark, he was left with no
　　other words.

STANLEY YOUNG

The Vikings — Scandinavian pirates and warriors who terrorized Europe from the eighth to the eleventh century — were known for their wild behavior, their heavy drinking, and their habit of seizing whatever they wanted, by violent means if necessary. "The Skeleton in Armor" was inspired by the discovery, in Massachusetts, of a most unusual grave. The remains in the grave appeared to be those of a Viking warrior. Longfellow invented this story to explain how the warrior came to be on this continent centuries before Columbus.

THE SKELETON IN ARMOR

"Speak! speak! thou fearful guest!
   Who, with thy hollow breast
Still in rude armor drest,
   Comest to daunt me!
Wrapt not in Eastern balms
But with thy fleshless palms
Stretched, as if asking alms,
   Why dost thou haunt me?"

Then, from those cavernous eyes
Pale flashes seemed to rise,
As when the Northern skies
   Gleam in December;
And, like the water's flow
Under December's snow,
Came a dull voice of woe
   From the heart's chamber.

"I was a Viking old!
My deeds, though manifold,
No Skald in song has told,
   No Saga taught thee!
Take heed, that in thy verse
Thou dost the tale rehearse,

Else dread a dead man's curse;
   For this I sought thee.

"Far in the Northern Land,
By the wild Baltic's strand,
I, with my childish hand,
   Tamed the gerfalcon;
And, with my skates fast-bound,
Skimmed the half-frozen Sound,
That the poor whimpering hound
   Trembled to walk on.

"Oft to his frozen lair
Tracked I the grisly bear,
While from my path the hare
   Fled like a shadow;
Oft through the forest dark
Followed the werewolf's bark,
Until the soaring lark
   Sang from the meadow.

"But when I older grew,
Joining a corsair's crew,
O'er the dark sea I flew
   With the marauders.
Wild was the life we led;
Many the souls that sped,
Many the hearts that bled,
   By our stern orders.

"Many a wassail-bout
Wore the long Winter out;
Often our midnight shout
   Set the cocks crowing,

As we the Berserk's tale
Measured in cups of ale,
Draining the oaken pail,
   Filled to o'erflowing.

"Once as I told in glee
Tales of the stormy sea,
Soft eyes did gaze on me,
   Burning yet tender;
And as the white stars shine
On the dark Norway pine,
On that dark heart of mine
   Fell their soft splendor.

"I wooed the blue-eyed maid,
Yielding, yet half afraid,
And in the forest's shade
   Our vows were plighted.
Under its loosened vest
Fluttered her little breast,
Like birds within their nest
   By the hawk frighted.

"Bright in her father's hall
Shields gleamed upon the wall,
Loud sang the minstrels all,
   Chanting his glory;
When of old Hildebrand
I asked his daughter's hand,
Mute did the minstrels stand
   To hear my story.

"While the brown ale he quaffed,
Loud then the champion laughed,

And as the wind-gusts waft
    The sea-foam brightly,
So the loud laugh of scorn,
Out of those lips unshorn,
From the deep drinking-horn
    Blew the foam lightly.

"She was a Prince's child,
I but a Viking wild,
And though she blushed and smiled,
    I was discarded!
Should not the dove so white
Follow the sea-mew's flight,
Why did they leave that night
    Her nest unguarded?

"Scarce had I put to sea,
Bearing the maid with me,
Fairest of all was she
    Among the Norsemen!
When on the white sea-strand,
Waving his armèd hand,
Saw we old Hildebrand,
    With twenty horsemen.

"Then launched they to the blast,
Bent like a reed each mast,
Yet we were gaining fast,
    When the wind failed us;
And with a sudden flaw
Came round the gusty Skaw,
So that our foe we saw
    Laugh as he hailed us.

"And as to catch the gale
Round veered the flapping sail,
'Death!' was the helmsman's hail,
   'Death without quarter!'
Mid-ships with iron keel
Struck we her ribs of steel;
Down her black hulk did reel
   Through the black water!

"As with his wings aslant,
Sails the fierce cormorant,
Seeking some rocky haunt,
   With his prey laden —
So toward the open main,
Beating to sea again,
Through the wild hurricane,
   Bore I the maiden.

"Three weeks we westward bore,
And when the storm was o'er,
Cloudlike we saw the shore
   Stretching to leeward;
There for my lady's bower
Built I the lofty tower,
Which, to this very hour,
   Stands looking seaward.

"There lived we many years;
Time dried the maiden's tears;
She had forgot her fears,
   She was a mother;
Death closed her mild blue eyes,
Under that tower she lies;
Ne'er shall the sun arise
   On such another!

"Still grew my bosom then,
Still as a stagnant fen!
Hateful to me were men,
    The sunlight hateful!
In the vast forest here,
Clad in my warlike gear,
Fell I upon my spear,
    Oh, death was grateful!

"Thus, seamed with many scars,
Bursting these prison bars,
Up to its native stars
    My soul ascended!
There from the flowing bowl
Deep drinks the warrior's soul,
Skoal! To the Northland! *Skoal!*"
    Thus the tale ended.

HENRY WADSWORTH LONGFELLOW

According to the legend on which this poem is based, when Confederate troops commanded by General Stonewall Jackson marched into Frederick, Maryland, only one inhabitant had the courage to hang out the Union flag, the Stars and Stripes. That brave citizen was ninety-year-old Barbara Frietchie. You'll notice that the poet, although obviously convinced that the Northern cause was right, nevertheless portrays Stonewall Jackson favorably, as a gentleman and a model of Southern gallantry.

BARBARA FRIETCHIE

Up from the meadows rich with corn,
Clear in the cool September morn,

The clustered spires of Frederick stand
Green-walled by the hills of Maryland.

Round about them orchards sweep,
Apple and peach tree fruited deep,

Fair as the garden of the Lord
To the eyes of the famished rebel horde,

On that pleasant morn of the early fall
When Lee marched over the mountain wall;

Over the mountains winding down,
Horse and foot, into Frederick town.

Forty flags with their silver stars,
Forty flags with their crimson bars,

Flapped in the morning wind: the sun
Of noon looked down, and saw not one.

Up rose old Barbara Frietchie then,
Bowed with her fourscore years and ten;

Bravest of all in Frederick town,
She took up the flag the men hauled down;

In her attic window the staff she set,
To show that one heart was loyal yet.

Up the street came the rebel tread.
Stonewall Jackson riding ahead.

Under his slouched hat left and right
He glanced; the old flag met his sight.

"Halt!" — the dust-brown ranks stood fast,
"Fire" — out blazed the rifle-blast.

It shivered the window, pane and sash;
It rent the banner with seam and gash.

Quick as it fell, from the broken staff
Dame Barbara snatched the silken scarf.

She leaned far out on the window-sill,
And shook it forth with a royal will.

"Shoot, if you must, this old gray head,
But spare your country's flag," she said.

A shade of sadness, a blush of shame,
Over the face of the leader came;

The nobler nature within him stirred
To life at that woman's deed and word;

"Who touches a hair of yon gray head
Dies like a dog! March on!" he said.

All day long through Frederick street
Sounded the tread of marching feet:

All day long that free flag tossed
Over the heads of the rebel host.

Ever its torn folds rose and fell
On the loyal winds that loved it well;

And through the hill-gaps sunset light
Shone over it with a warm good-night.

Barbara Frietchie's work is o'er,
And the Rebel rides on his raids no more.

Honor to her! And let a tear
Fall, for her sake, on Stonewall's bier.

Over Barbara Frietchie's grave,
Flag of Freedom and Union, wave!

Peace and order and beauty draw
Round thy symbol of light and law;

And ever the stars above look down
On thy stars below in Frederick town!

JOHN GREENLEAF WHITTIER

There was a time when travelers on English roads lived in constant fear of being stopped and robbed by highwaymen. Naturally, they regarded these highway robbers as criminals. In this poem, however, Alfred Noyes gives us a different view. His highwayman is a romantic, dashing figure who eventually gains our sympathy, if not our approval.

THE HIGHWAYMAN

PART ONE

The wind was a torrent of darkness among the gusty trees,
The moon was a ghostly galleon tossed upon cloudy seas,
The road was a ribbon of moonlight over the purple moor,
And the highwayman came riding —
      Riding — riding —
The highwayman came riding, up to the old inn-door.

He'd a French cocked-hat on his forehead, a bunch of lace
    at his chin,
A coat of the claret velvet, and breeches of brown doeskin:
They fitted with never a wrinkle; his boots were up to the
    thigh!
And he rode with a jewelled twinkle,
      His pistol butts a-twinkle,
His rapier hilt a-twinkle, under the jewelled sky.

Over the cobbles he clattered and clashed in the dark inn-
    yard,
And he tapped with his whip on the shutters, but all was
    locked and barred:
He whistled a tune to the window, and who should be
    waiting there
But the landlord's black-eyed daughter,
      Bess, the landlord's daughter,
Plaiting a dark red love-knot into her long black hair.

And dark in the dark old inn-yard a stable-wicket creaked
Where Tim, the ostler, listened; his face was white and
    peaked,
His eyes were hollows of madness, his hair like moldy hay;
But he loved the landlord's daughter,
        The landlord's red-lipped daughter:
Dumb as a dog he listened, and he heard the robber say —

"One kiss, my bonny sweetheart, I'm after a prize tonight,
But I shall be back with the yellow gold before the morning
    light.
Yet if they press me sharply, and harry me through the day,
Then look for me by moonlight:
        Watch for me by moonlight:
I'll come to thee by moonlight, though Hell should bar the
    way."

He rose upright in the stirrups, he scarce could reach her
    hand;
But she loosened her hair i' the casement! His face burnt
    like a brand
As the black cascade of perfume came tumbling over his
    breast;
And he kissed its waves in the moonlight,
        (Oh, sweet black waves in the moonlight)
Then he tugged at his reins in the moonlight, and galloped
    away to the West.

PART TWO

He did not come in the dawning; he did not come at noon;
And out of the tawny sunset, before the rise o' the moon,
When the road was a gypsy's ribbon, looping the purple
     moor,
A red-coat troop came marching —
          Marching — marching —
King George's men came marching, up to the old inn-door.

They said no word to the landlord, they drank his ale
     instead;
But they gagged his daughter and bound her to the foot of
     her narrow bed.
Two of them knelt at her casement, with muskets at the
     side!
There was death at every window;
          And Hell at one dark window;
For Bess could see, through her casement, the road that *he*
     would ride.

They had tied her up to attention, with many a sniggering
     jest:
They had bound a musket beside her, with the barrel
     beneath her breast!
"Now keep good watch!" and they kissed her.
          She heard the dead man say —
Look for me by moonlight;
          Watch for me by moonlight;
I'll come to thee by moonlight, though Hell should bar the way!

She twisted her hands behind her; but all the knots held
    good!
She writhed her hands till her fingers were wet with sweat
    or blood!
They stretched and strained in the darkness, and the hours
    crawled by like years;
Till, now, on the stroke of midnight,
        Cold, on the stroke of midnight,
The tip of one finger touched it! The trigger at least was
    hers!

The tip of one finger touched it; she strove no more for the
    rest!
Up, she stood up to attention, with the barrel beneath her
    breast,
She would not risk their hearing; she would not strive
    again;
For the road lay bare in the moonlight,
        Blank and bare in the moonlight;
And the blood of her veins in the moonlight throbbed to
    her Love's refrain.

Tlot-tlot, tlot-tlot! Had they heard it? The horse-hoofs
    ringing clear —
Tlot-tlot, tlot-tlot, in the distance? Were they deaf that they
    did not hear?
Down the ribbon of moonlight, over the brow of the hill,
The highwayman came riding,
        Riding, riding!
The red-coats looked to their priming! She stood up
    straight and still!
Tlot-tlot, in the frosty silence! *Tlot-tlot,* in the echoing night!
Nearer he came and nearer! Her face was like a light!

Her eyes grew wide for a moment; she drew one last deep
    breath,
Then her finger moved in the moonlight,
        Her musket shattered the moonlight,
Shattered her breast in the moonlight and warned him —
    with her death.

He turned; he spurred him Westward; he did not know
    who stood
Bowed with her head o'er the musket, drenched with her
    own red blood!
Not till the dawn he heard it, and slowly blanched to hear
How Bess, the landlord's daughter,
        The landlord's black-eyed daughter,
Had watched for her Love in the moonlight; and died in
    the darkness there.

Back, he spurred like a madman, shrieking a curse to the
    sky,
With the white road smoking behind him, and his rapier
    brandished high!
Blood-red were his spurs i' the golden noon; wine-red was
    his velvet coat;
When they shot him down on the highway,
        Down like a dog on the highway,
And he lay in his blood on the highway, with the bunch of
    lace at his throat.

And still a winter's night, they say, when the wind is in the trees,
When the moon is a ghostly galleon tossed upon cloudy seas,
When the road is a ribbon of moonlight over the purple moor,
A highwayman comes riding —
        Riding — riding —
A highwayman comes riding, up to the old inn-door.

Over the cobbles he clatters and clangs in the dark inn-yard;
And he taps with his whip on the shutters, but all is locked and
*   barred:*
He whistles a tune to the window, and who should be waiting
*   there*
But the landlord's black-eyed daughter,
*   Bess, the landlord's daughter,*
Plaiting a dark red love-knot into her long black hair.

ALFRED NOYES

A great American naval captain of the Revolutionary War was John Paul Jones. On September 23, 1779, he fought his most important sea battle, against a far superior British fleet. The British ships seemed invincible; yet, even when his ship began to sink, Jones refused to surrender.

AN OLD-TIME SEA-FIGHT

Would you hear of an old-time sea-fight?
Would you learn who won by the light of the moon and
    stars?
List to the yarn, as my grandmother's father the sailor told
    it to me.

Our foe was no skulk in his ship I tell you (said he),
His was the surly English pluck, and there is no tougher or
    truer, and never was and never will be;
Along the lower'd eve he came horribly raking us.

We closed with him, the yards entangled, the cannon
    touch'd,
My captain lash'd fast with his own hands.

We had receiv'd some eighteen pound shots under the
    water;
On our lower gun-deck two large pieces had burst at the
    first fire, killing all around and blowing up overhead.

Fighting at sun-down, fighting at dark,
Ten o'clock at night, the full moon well up, our leaks on the
    gain, and five feet of water reported,
The master-at-arms loosing the prisoners confined in the
    after hold to give them a chance for themselves.

The transit to and from the magazine is now stopt by the
    sentinels,
They see so many strange faces they do not know whom to
    trust.

Our frigate takes fire,
The other asks if we demand quarter?
If our colours are struck and the fighting done?

Now I laugh content, for I hear the voice of my little
    captain,
We have not struck, he composedly cries, *we have just begun
    our part of the fighting.*

Only three guns are in use,
One is directed by the captain himself against the enemy's
    main-mast,
Two well serv'd with grape and canister silence his
    musketry and clear his decks.

The tops alone second the fire of this little battery,
    especially the main-top,
They hold out bravely during the whole of the action.

Not a moment's cease,
The leaks gain fast on the pumps, the fire eats toward the
    powder-magazine.

One of the pumps has been shot away, it is generally
    thought we are sinking.

Serene stands the little captain,
He is not hurried, his voice is neither high nor low,
His eyes give more light to us than our battle-lanterns.

Toward twelve there in the beams of the moon they
    surrender to us.

WALT WHITMAN

During the reign of King Francis I of France (1515-1547), lion fights were a favorite royal entertainment, a knight's honor was his most precious possession, and a lady's glove was the symbol of her favor.

THE GLOVE AND THE LIONS

King Francis was a hearty king, and loved a royal sport,
And one day, as his lions fought, sat looking on the court.
The nobles fill'd the benches, with the ladies in their pride,
And 'mongst them sat the Count de Lorge, with one for
    whom he sigh'd:
And truly 'twas a gallant thing to see that crowning show,
Valor and love, and a king above, and the royal beasts
    below.

Ramp'd and roar'd the lions, with horrid laughing jaws;
They bit, they glared, gave blows like beams, a wind went
    with their paws,
With wallowing might and stifled roar they roll'd on one
    another,
Till all the pit with sand and mane was in a thunderous
    smother;
The bloody foam above the bars came whisking through
    the air;
Said Francis then, "Faith, gentlemen, we're better here
    than there."
De Lorge's love o'erheard the king, a beauteous, lively
    dame,
With smiling lips and sharp bright eyes, which always
    seem'd the same;
She thought, The Count my lover is brave as brave can be;
He surely would do wondrous things to show his love of
    me;

King, ladies, lovers, all look on; the occasion is divine;
I'll drop my glove, to prove his love; great glory will be
    mine.

She dropp'd her glove, to prove his love, then look'd at him
    and smiled;
He bow'd, and in a moment leap'd among the lions wild;
The leap was quick, return was quick, he has regain'd his
    place,
Then threw the glove, but not with love, right in the lady's
    face.
"By heaven," said Francis, "rightly done!" and he rose from
    where he sat;
"No love," quoth he, "but vanity, sets love a task like that."

LEIGH HUNT

Napoleon Bonaparte, a brilliant military leader and Emperor of France from 1804 to 1814, was immensely popular with his soldiers. In 1809, when his troops stormed Ratisbon (now Regensburg, in West Germany), Napoleon was at the height of his power. The officers and men of his army served him with a devotion that verged on worship.

INCIDENT OF THE FRENCH CAMP

You know, we French stormed Ratisbon.
   A mile or so away,
On a little mound, Napoleon
   Stood on our storming-day;
With neck out-thrust, you fancy how,
   Legs wide, arms locked behind,
As if to balance the prone brow
   Oppressive with its mind.

Just as perhaps he mused "My plans
   That soar, to earth may fall,
Let once my army-leader Lannes
   Waver at yonder wall" —
Out 'twixt the battery smokes there flew
   A rider, bound on bound
Full-galloping, nor bridle drew
   Until he reached the mound.

Then off there flung in smiling joy,
   And held himself erect
By just his horse's mane, a boy:
   You hardly could suspect —
(So tight he kept his lips compressed,
   Scarce any blood came through)
You looked twice ere you saw his breast
   Was all but shot in two.

"Well," cried he, "Emperor, by God's grace
    We've got you Ratisbon!
The Marshal's in the market-place,
    And you'll be there anon
To see your flag-bird flap his vans
    Where I, to heart's desire,
Perched him!" The chief's eye flashed; his plans
    Soared up again like fire.

The chief's eye flashed; but presently
    Softened itself, as sheathes
A film the mother-eagle's eye
    When her bruised eaglet breathes;
"You're wounded!" "Nay," the soldier's pride
    Touched to the quick, he said:
"I'm killed, Sire!" And, his chief beside,
    Smiling, the boy fell dead.

ROBERT BROWNING

When the Nazis invaded France in 1940, British troops who had been
fighting alongside their French allies were driven north to the port of
Dunkirk. There they were trapped, their only hope being to find some way
to escape across the English Channel. More than 250,000 men would have
perished had not the British people sent a flotilla of fishing boats, yachts,
little pleasure craft — anything at all that would float — to rescue them.

DUNKIRK

Will came back from school that day,
And he had little to say.
But he stood a long time looking down
To where the gray-green Channel water
Slapped at the foot of the little town,
And to where his boat, the *Sarah P,*
Bobbed at the tide on an even keel,
With her one old sail, patched at the leech,
Furled like a slattern down at heel.

He stood for a while above the beach;
He saw how the wind and current caught her.
He looked a long time out to sea.
There was steady wind and the sky was pale,
And a haze in the east that looked like smoke.

Will went back to the house to dress.
He was halfway through when his sister Bess,
Who was near fourteen and younger than he
By just two years, came home from play.
She asked him, "Where are you going, Will?"
He said, "For a good long sail."
"Can I come along?"
             "No, Bess," he spoke.
"I may be gone for a night and a day."
Bess looked at him. She kept very still.

She had heard the news of the Flanders rout,
How the English were trapped above Dunkirk,
And the fleet had gone to get them out —
But everyone thought that it wouldn't work.
There was too much to fear, there was too much doubt.

She looked at him and he looked at her.
They were English children, born and bred.
He frowned her down, but she wouldn't stir.
She shook her proud head.
"You'll need a crew," she said.

They raised the sail on the *Sarah P,*
Like a penoncel on a young knight's lance,
And headed the *Sarah* out to sea,
To bring their soldiers home from France.

There was no command, there was no set plan,
But six hundred boats went out with them
On the gray-green waters, sailing fast,
River excursion and fisherman,
Tug and schooner and racing M,
And the little boats came following last.

From every harbor and town they went
Who had sailed their craft in the sun and rain,
From the South Downs, from the cliffs of Kent,
From the village street, from the country lane.
There are twenty miles of rolling sea
From coast to coast, by the seagull's flight.
But the tides were fair and the wind was free,
And they raised Dunkirk by the fall of night.

They raised Dunkirk with its harbor torn
By the blasted stern and the sunken prow;
They had raced for fun on an English tide,
They were English children bred and born,
And whether they lived or whether they died,
They raced for England now.

Bess was as white as the *Sarah's* sail,
She set her teeth and smiled at Will.
He held his course for the smoky veil
Where the harbor narrowed thin and long.
The British ships were firing strong.

He took the *Sarah* into his hands,
He drove her in through fire and death
To the wet men waiting on the sands.
He got his load and he got his breath,
And she came about, and the wind fought her.
He shut his eyes and he tried to pray.
He saw his England where she lay,
The wind's green home, the sea's proud daughter.
Still in the moonlight, dreaming deep,
The English cliffs and the English loam —
He had fourteen men to get away,
And the moon was clear and the night like day
For planes to see where the white sails creep
Over the black water.

He closed his eyes and he prayed for her;
He prayed to the men who had made her great,
Who had built her land of forest and park,
Who had made the seas an English lake;
He prayed for a fog to bring the dark;
He prayed to get home for England's sake.

And the fog came down on the rolling sea,
And covered the ships with English mist.
The diving planes were baffled and blind.
For Nelson was there in the *Victory*,
With his one good eye, and his sullen twist,
And guns were out on *The Golden Hind*,
Their shot flashed over the *Sarah P.*
He could hear them cheer as he came about.

By burning wharves, by battered slips,
Galleon, frigate, and brigantine,
The old dead Captains fought their ships,
And the great dead Admirals led the line.
It was England's night, it was England's sea.

The fog rolled over the harbor key.
Bess held to the stays and conned him out.

And all through the dark, while the *Sarah's* wake
Hissed behind him, and vanished in foam,
There at his side sat Francis Drake,
And held him true and steered him home.

ROBERT NATHAN

GROUP 2

FUN

AND

FANTASY

THE TWINS

In form and feature, face and limb,
   I grew so like my brother,
That folks got taking me for him,
   And each for one another.
It puzzled all our kith and kin,
   It reached a fearful pitch;
For one of us was born a twin,
   Yet not a soul knew which.

One day, to make the matter worse,
   Before our names were fixed,
As we were being washed by nurse,
   We got completely mixed;
And thus, you see, by fate's decree,
   Or rather nurse's whim,
My brother John got christened me,
   And I got christened him.

This fatal likeness even dogged
   My footsteps when at school,
And I was always getting flogged,
   For John turned out a fool.
I put this question, fruitlessly,
   To everyone I knew,
"What *would* you do, if you were me,
   To prove that you were *you?*"

Our close resemblance turned the tide
  Of my domestic life,
For somehow, my intended bride
  Became my brother's wife.
In fact, year after year the same
  Absurd mistakes went on,
And when I died, the neighbors came
  And buried brother John.

HENRY SAMBROOKE LEIGH

BIOGRAPHIES

1

NOW this is the story of Lucy Brown,
A glittering jewel in virtue's crown.
From earliest youth, she aspired to please.
She never fell down and dirtied her knees;
She put all her pennies in savings banks;
She never omitted her "please" and "thanks";
She swallowed her spinach without a squawk;
And patiently listened to Teacher's talk;
She thoughtfully stepped over worms and ants;
And earnestly watered the potted plants;
She didn't dismember expensive toys;
And never would play with the little boys.

And when to young womanhood Lucy came
Her mode of behavior was just the same.
She always was safe in her home at dark;
And never went riding around the park;
She wouldn't put powder upon her nose;
And petticoats sheltered her spotless hose;
She knew how to market and mend and sweep;
By quarter-past ten, she was sound asleep;
In presence of elders, she held her tongue —
The way that they did when the world was young.
And people remarked, in benign accord,
"You'll see that she gathers her just reward."

Observe, their predictions were more than fair.
She married an affluent millionaire
So gallant and handsome and wise and gay,
And rated in Bradstreet at Double A.
And she lived with him happily all her life,
And made him a perfectly elegant wife.

2

Now Marigold Jones, from her babyhood,
Was bad as the model Miss Brown was good.
She stuck out her tongue at her grieving nurse;
She frequently rifled her Grandma's purse;
She banged on the table and broke the plates;
She jeered at the passing inebriates;
And tore all her dresses and ripped her socks;
And shattered the windows with fair-sized rocks;
The words on the fences she'd memorize;
She blackened her dear little brother's eyes;
And cut off her sister's abundant curls;
And never would play with the little girls.

And when she grew up — as is hardly strange —
Her manner of life underwent no change
But faithfully followed her childhood plan.
And once there was talk of a married man!
She sauntered in public in draperies
Affording no secrecy to her knees;
She constantly uttered what was not true;
She flirted and petted, or what have you;
And, tendered advice by her kind Mamma,
Her answer, I shudder to state, was "Blah!"
And people remarked, in sepulchral tones,
"You'll see what becomes of Marigold Jones."

Observe, their predictions were more than fair.
She married an affluent millionaire
So gallant and handsome and wise and gay,
And rated in Bradstreet at Double A.
And she lived with him happily all her life,
And made him a perfectly elegant wife.

DOROTHY PARKER

THE FROGS WHO WANTED A KING

The frogs were living happy as could be
   In a wet marsh to which they all were suited;
From every sort of trouble they were free,
   And all night long they croaked, and honked, and
      hooted.
But one fine day a bull-frog said, "The thing
We never had and *must* have is a king."

So all the frogs immediately prayed;
   "Great Jove," they chorused from their swampy border,
"Send us a king and he will be obeyed,
   A king to bring a rule of Law and Order."
Jove heard and chuckled. That night in the bog
There fell a long and most impressive Log.

The swamp was silent; nothing breathed. At first
   The badly frightened frogs did never *once* stir;
But gradually some neared and even durst
   To touch, aye, even dance upon, the monster.
Whereat they croaked again, "Great Jove, oh hear!
Send us a *living* king, a king to fear."

Once more Jove smiled, and sent them down a Stork,
   "Long live — !" they croaked. But ere they framed the
      sentence,
The Stork bent down and, scorning knife and fork,
   Swallowed them all, with no time for repentance!

THE MORAL'S this: No matter what your lot,
It might be worse. Be glad with what you've got.

JOSEPH LAUREN

THE YARN OF THE NANCY BELL

'Twas on the shores that round our coast
   From Deal to Ramsgate span,
That I found alone on a piece of stone,
   An elderly naval man.

His hair was weedy, his beard was long,
   And weedy and long was he;
And I heard this wight on the shore recite
   In a singular minor key:

"Oh, I am a cook and a captain bold,
   And the mate of the Nancy brig,
And a bo'sun tight, and a midshipmite,
   And the crew of the captain's gig."

And he shook his fists and he tore his hair,
   Till I really felt afraid,
For I couldn't help thinking the man had been drinking,
   And so I simply said:

"O elderly man, it's little I know
   Of the duties of men of the sea,
And I'll eat my hand if I understand
   How ever you can be

"At once a cook and a captain bold,
   And the mate of the Nancy brig,
And a bo'sun tight, and a midshipmite,
   And the crew of the captain's gig!"

Then he gave a hitch to his trousers, which
    Is a trick all seamen larn,
And having got rid of a thumping quid,
    He spun this painful yarn:

" 'Twas in the good ship Nancy Bell
    That we sail'd to the Indian sea,
And there on a reef we come to grief,
    Which has often occurr'd to me.

"And pretty nigh all o' the crew was drown'd
    (There was seventy-seven o' soul);
And only ten of the Nancy's men
    Said 'Here!' to the muster-roll.

"There was me, and the cook, and the captain bold,
    And the mate of the Nancy brig,
And the bo'sun tight and a midshipmite,
    And the crew of the captain's gig.

"For a month we'd neither vittles nor drink,
    Till a-hungry we did feel,
So we draw'd a lot, and, accordin', shot
    The captain for our meal.

"The next lot fell to the Nancy's mate,
    And a delicate dish he made;
Then our appetite with the midshipmite
    We seven survivors stay'd.

"And then we murder'd the bo'sun tight,
    And he much resembled pig;
Then we vittled free, did the cook and me,
    On the crew of the captain's gig.

"Then only the cook and me was left,
   And the delicate question, 'Which
Of us two goes to the kettle?' arose,
   And we argued it out as sich.

"For I loved that cook as a brother, I did,
   And the cook he worship'd me;
But we'd both be blow'd if we'd either be stow'd
   In the other chap's hold, you see.

"'I'll be eat if you dines off me,' says Tom,
   'Yes, that,' says I, 'you'll be.
I'm boil'd if I die, my friend,' quoth I;
   And 'Exactly so,' quoth he.

"Says he: 'Dear James, to murder me
   Were a foolish thing to do,
For don't you see that you can't cook *me*,
   While I can — and will — cook *you?*'

"So he boils the water, and takes the salt
   And the pepper in portions true
(Which he never forgot), and some chopp'd shallot,
   And some sage and parsley too.

"'Come here,' says he, with a proper pride,
   Which his smiling features tell:
''Twill soothing be if I let you see
   How extremely nice you'll smell.'

"And he stirr'd it round and round and round,
   And he sniff'd at the foaming froth;
When I ups with his heels, and smothers his squeals
   In the scum of the boiling broth.

"And I eat that cook in a week or less,
    And as I eating be
The last of his chops, why I almost drops,
    For a vessel in sight I see.

"And I never larf, and I never smile,
    And I never lark nor play;
But I sit and croak, and a single joke
    I have — which is to say:

"Oh, I am a cook and a captain bold,
    And the mate of the Nancy brig,
And a bo'sun tight, and a midshipmite,
    And the crew of the captain's gig!"

WILLIAM SCHWENCK GILBERT

THE WALRUS AND THE CARPENTER

The sun was shining on the sea,
   Shining with all his might:
He did his very best to make
   The billows smooth and bright —
And this was odd, because it was
   The middle of the night.

The moon was shining sulkily,
   Because she thought the sun
Had got no business to be there
   After the day was done —
"It's very rude of him," she said,
   "To come and spoil the fun!"

The sea was wet as wet could be,
   The sands were dry as dry.
You could not see a cloud, because
   No cloud was in the sky:
No birds were flying overhead —
   There were no birds to fly.

The Walrus and the Carpenter
   Were walking close at hand:
They wept like anything to see
   Such quantities of sand.
"If this were only cleared away,"
   They said, "it *would* be grand!"

"If seven maids with seven mops
 Swept it for half a year,
Do you suppose," the Walrus said,
 "That they could get it clear?"
"I doubt it," said the Carpenter,
 And shed a bitter tear.

"O Oysters, come and walk with us!"
 The Walrus did beseech.
"A pleasant walk, a pleasant talk,
 Along the briny beach:
We cannot do with more than four,
 To give a hand to each."

The eldest Oyster looked at him,
 But never a word he said:
The eldest Oyster winked his eye,
 And shook his heavy head —
Meaning to say he did not choose
 To leave the oyster bed.

But four young Oysters hurried up,
 All eager for the treat:
Their coats were brushed, their faces washed,
 Their shoes were clean and neat —
And this was odd, because, you know,
 They hadn't any feet.

Four other Oysters followed them.
    And yet another four;
And thick and fast they came at last,
    And more, and more, and more —
All hopping through the frothy waves,
    And scrambling to the shore.

The Walrus and the Carpenter
    Walked on a mile or so,
And then they rested on a rock
    Conveniently low.
And all the little Oysters stood
    And waited in a row.

"The time has come," the Walrus said,
    "To talk of many things:
Of shoes — and ships — and sealing-wax —
    Of cabbages — and kings —
And why the sea is boiling hot —
    And whether pigs have wings."

"But wait a bit," the Oysters cried,
    "Before we have our chat;
For some of us are out of breath,
    And all of us are fat!"
"No hurry!" said the Carpenter.
    They thanked him much for that.

"A loaf of bread," the Walrus said,
    "Is what we chiefly need:
Pepper and vinegar, besides,
    Are very good indeed —
Now, if you're ready, Oysters dear,
    We can begin to feed."

"But not on us!" the Oysters cried,
    Turning a little blue.
"After such kindness, that would be
    A dismal thing to do!"
"The night is fine," the Walrus said,
    "Do you admire the view?"

"It was so kind of you to come!
    And you are very nice!"
The Carpenter said nothing but
    "Cut us another slice:
I wish you were not quite so deaf —
    I've had to ask you twice!"

"It seems a shame," the Walrus said,
    "To play them such a trick,
After we've brought them out so far,
    And made them trot so quick!"
The carpenter said nothing but
    "The butter's spread too thick!"

"I weep for you," the Walrus said:
    "I deeply sympathize."
With sobs and tears he sorted out
    Those of the largest size,
Holding his pocket-handkerchief
    Before his streaming eyes.

"O Oysters," said the Carpenter,
    "You've had a pleasant run!
Shall we be trotting home again?"
    But answer came there none —
And this was scarcely odd, because
    They'd eaten every one.

LEWIS CARROLL

When gold was discovered in Alaska in 1896, thousands from all over the country left their families, their businesses, and sometimes their common sense to "moil" (work hard in the dirt) for gold in that frozen land. Some made as much as $5,000 in three days, but many more perished from hunger, disease, or the bitter cold.

THE CREMATION OF SAM McGEE

There are strange things done in the midnight sun
  By the men who moil for gold;
The Arctic trails have their secret tales
  That would make your blood run cold;
The northern lights have seen queer sights,
  But the queerest they ever did see
Was that night on the marge of Lake Lebarge
  I cremated Sam McGee.

Now Sam McGee was from Tennessee, where the cotton
  blooms and blows.
Why he left his home in the South to roam 'round the pole,
  God only knows.
He was always cold, but the land of gold seemed to hold
  him like a spell,
Though he'd often say in his homely way that he'd sooner
  live in hell.

On Christmas Day we were mushing our way over the
  Dawson Trail.
Talk of your cold! Through the parka's fold it stabbed like a
  driven nail.
If our eyes we'd close, then the lashes froze till sometimes
  we couldn't see;
It wasn't much fun, but the only one to whimper was Sam
  McGee.

And that very night, as we lay packed tight in our robes
  beneath the snow,
And the dogs were fed, and the stars o'erhead were
  dancing heel and toe,
He turned to me, and "Cap," says he, "I'll cash in this trip, I
  guess;
And if I do, I'm asking that you won't refuse my last
  request."

Well, he seemed so low that I couldn't say no; then he says
  with a sort of moan:
"It's the cursèd cold, and it's got right hold till I'm chilled
  clean through to the bone.
Yet 'taint being dead — it's my awful dread of the icy grave
  that pains;
So I want you to swear that, foul or fair, you'll cremate my
  last remains."

A pal's last need is a thing to heed, so I swore I would not
  fail;
And we started on at the streak of dawn; but God! he
  looked ghastly pale.
He crouched on the sleigh, and he raved all day of his
  home in Tennessee;
And before nightfall a corpse was all that was left of Sam
  McGee.

There wasn't a breath in that land of death, and I hurried,
  horror-driven,
With a corpse half hid that I couldn't get rid, because of a
  promise I'd given;
It was lashed to the sleigh, and it seemed to say: "You may
  tax your brawn and brains,

But you promised true, and it's up to you to cremate those
    last remains."

Now a promise made is a debt unpaid, and the trail has its
    own stern code;
In the days to come, though my lips were dumb, in my
    heart how I cursed that load.
In the long, long night, by the lone firelight, while the
    huskies, 'round in a ring,
Howled out their woes to the homeless snows — O God!
    how I loathed the thing.

And every day that quiet clay seemed to heavy and heavier
    grow;
And on I went, though the dogs were spent and the grub
    was getting low;
The trail was bad, and I felt half mad, but I swore I would
    not give in;
And I'd often sing to the hateful thing, and it harkened
    with a grin.

Till I came to the marge of Lake Lebarge, and a derelict
    there lay;
It was jammed in the ice, but I saw in a trice it was called
    the Alice May.
And I looked at it, and I thought a bit, and I looked at my
    frozen chum;
Then "Here," said I, with a sudden cry, "is my cre-ma-tor-
    i-um."

Some planks I tore from the cabin floor, and I lit the boiler
    fire;
Some coal I found that was lying around, and I heaped the
    fuel higher;

The flames just soared, and the furnace roared — such a
   blaze you seldom see;
And I burrowed a hole in the glowing coal, and I stuffed in
   Sam McGee.

Then I made a hike, for I didn't like to hear him sizzle so;
And the heavens scowled, and the huskies howled, and the
   wind began to blow.
It was icy cold, but the hot sweat rolled down my cheeks,
   and I don't know why;
And the greasy smoke in an inky cloak went streaking
   down the sky.

I do not know how long in the snow I wrestled with grisly
   fear;
But the stars came out and they danced about 'ere again I
   ventured near;
I was sick with dread, but I bravely said: "I'll just take a
   peep inside.
I guess he's cooked, and it's time I looked" . . . then the
   door I opened wide.

And there sat Sam, looking cold and calm, in the heart of
   the furnace roar;
And he wore a smile you could see a mile, and he said,
   "Please close that door!
It's fine in here, but I greatly fear you'll let in the cold and
   storm —
Since I left Plumtree, down in Tennessee, it's the first time
   I've been warm."

There are strange things done in the midnight sun
   By the men who moil for gold;
The Arctic trails have their secret tales
   That would make your blood run cold;
The northern lights have seen queer sights,
   But the queerest they ever did see
Was that night on the marge of Lake Lebarge
   I cremated Sam McGee.

ROBERT W. SERVICE

ADVENTURES OF ISABEL

Isabel met an enormous bear;
Isabel, Isabel, didn't care.
The bear was hungry, the bear was ravenous,
The bear's big mouth was cruel and cavernous.
The bear said, Isabel, glad to meet you,
How do, Isabel, now I'll eat you!
Isabel, Isabel, didn't worry,
Isabel didn't scream or scurry.
She washed her hands and she straightened her hair up.
Then Isabel quietly ate the bear up.

Once on a night as black as pitch
Isabel met a wicked old witch.
The witch's face was cross and wrinkled,
The witch's gums with teeth were sprinkled.
Ho, ho, Isabel! the old witch crowed,
I'll turn you into an ugly toad!
Isabel, Isabel, didn't worry,
Isabel didn't scream or scurry.
She showed no rage and she showed no rancor,
But she turned the witch into milk and drank her.

Isabel met a hideous giant,
Isabel continued self-reliant.
The giant was hairy, the giant was horrid,
He had one eye in the middle of his forehead.
Good morning, Isabel, the giant said,
I'll grind your bones to make my bread.

Isabel, Isabel, didn't worry,
Isabel didn't scream or scurry.
She nibbled the zwieback that she always fed off,
And when it was gone, she cut the giant's head off.

Isabel met a troublesome doctor,
He punched and he poked till he really shocked her.
The doctor's talk was of coughs and chills
And the doctor's satchel bulged with pills.
The doctor said unto Isabel,
Swallow this, it will make you well.
Isabel, Isabel, didn't worry,
Isabel didn't scream or scurry.
She took those pills from the pill-concocter,
And Isabel calmly cured the doctor.

OGDEN NASH

MATILDA

WHO TOLD LIES, AND WAS BURNED TO DEATH

Matilda told such Dreadful Lies
It made one Gasp and Stretch one's Eyes;
Her Aunt, who from her Earliest Youth,
Had kept a Strict Regard for Truth,
Attempted to Believe Matilda:
The effort very nearly killed her,
And would have done so, had not She
Discovered this Infirmity.
For once, towards the Close of Day,
Matilda, growing tired of play,
And finding she was left alone,
Went tiptoe to the Telephone
And summoned the Immediate Aid
Of London's Noble Fire-Brigade.
Within an hour the Gallant Band
Were pouring in on every hand,
From Putney, Hackney Downs and Bow,
With Courage high and Hearts a-glow
They galloped, roaring through the Town,
"Matilda's House is Burning Down!"

Inspired by British Cheers and Loud
Proceeding from the Frenzied Crowd,
They ran their ladders through a score
Of windows on the Ball Room Floor.
And took Peculiar Pains to Souse
The Pictures up and down the House
Until Matilda's Aunt succeeded
In showing them they were not needed
And even then she had to pay
To get the Men to go away!

It happened that a few Weeks later
Her Aunt was off to the Theatre
To see that Interesting Play
The Second Mrs. Tanqueray.
She had refused to take her Niece
To hear this Entertaining Piece:
A Deprivation Just and Wise
To Punish her for Telling Lies.
That Night a Fire *did* break out —
You should have heard Matilda Shout!
You should have heard her Scream and Bawl,
And throw the window up and call
To People passing in the Street —
(The rapidly increasing Heat
Encouraging her to obtain
Their confidence) — but all in vain!
For every time She shouted "Fire!"
They only answered "Little Liar!"
And therefore when her Aunt returned
Matilda, and the House, were Burned.

HILAIRE BELLOC

71

In Through the Looking-Glass *(the sequel to* Alice in Wonderland*), Alice comes upon Humpty Dumpty, of nursery rhyme fame. He recites to her a nonsense poem that he has written, he says, "entirely for your amusement."*

HUMPTY DUMPTY'S SONG

In winter, when the fields are white,
I sing this song for your delight —
In spring, when woods are getting green,
I'll try and tell you what I mean:

In summer, when the days are long,
Perhaps you'll understand the song:
In autumn, when the leaves are brown,
Take pen and ink, and write it down.

I sent a message to the fish:
I told them, "This is what I wish."
The little fishes of the sea,
They sent an answer back to me.

The little fishes' answer was
"We cannot do it, Sir, because — "
I sent to them again to say
"It will be better to obey."

The fishes answered, with a grin,
"Why, what a temper you are in!"
I told them once, I told them twice:
They would not listen to advice.

I took a kettle large and new,
Fit for the deed I had to do.
My heart went hop, my heart went thump:
I filled the kettle at the pump.

Then someone came to me and said,
"The little fishes are in bed."
I said to him, I said it plain,
"Then you must wake them up again."

I said it very loud and clear:
I went and shouted in his ear.
But he was very stiff and proud:
He said, "You needn't shout so loud!"

And he was very proud and stiff:
He said: "I'd go and wake them, if — "
I took a corkscrew from the shelf:
I went to wake them up myself.

And when I found the door was locked,
I pulled and pushed and kicked and knocked.
And when I found the door was shut,
I tried to turn the handle, but —

There was a long pause.
"Is that all?" Alice timidly asked.
"That's all," said Humpty Dumpty. "Good-bye."

LEWIS CARROLL

GROUP 3
HEROES
AND
VILLAINS

The James gang, led by Jesse James and his brother Frank, was the most notorious band of outlaws in U.S. history. In the 1870's the brothers ranged freely around the Midwest, robbing banks and trains. They were no Robin Hoods — they stole from both rich and poor to give to themselves — but for some reason a number of people preferred to regard them as heroes. These people were outraged when Jesse, who was living under the assumed name of Thomas Howard to escape the law, was killed by a member of his own gang, Robert Ford.

JESSE JAMES

It was on a Wednesday night, the moon was shining bright,
    They robbed the Glendale train.
And the people they did say, for many miles away,
    'Twas the outlaws Frank and Jesse James.

Jesse had a wife to mourn for his life,
    Three children, they were brave;
'Twas a dirty little coward shot Mister Howard
    And laid Jesse James in his grave.

It was Robert Ford, the dirty little coward,
    It's a shame how he did behave,
For he ate of Jesse's bread and he slept in Jesse's bed,
    Then he laid Jesse James in his grave.

Jesse was a man, was a friend to the poor,
    He never left a man in pain,
And with his brother Frank he robbed the Gallatin bank,
    And then held up the Glendale train.

They went to the crossing not very far from there,
    And there they did the same;
And the agent on his knees he delivered up the keys
    To the outlaws Frank and Jesse James.

It was on a Saturday night, Jesse was at home
   Talking to his family brave,
When the thief and the coward, little Robert Ford,
   Laid Jesse James in his grave.

The people held their breath when they heard of Jesse's
      death,
   And wondered how he ever came to die;
'Twas one of the gang called little Robert Ford,
   That shot Jesse James on the sly.

Jesse went to rest with his hand on his breast;
   His killing was a disgrace;
He was born one day in the county of Clay,
   And he came from a solitary race.

ANONYMOUS

In the days before jet planes and space shuttles, the fastest-moving vehicle on earth was the locomotive. "Fireboys" fed coal into the engine's furnace to produce the steam that drove the wheels, and the engineer operated the train from his cabin. The ballad of Casey Jones is based on the true story of John Luther Jones, who, on April 30, 1906, was killed when his train plowed into the back of a freight train ahead of him on the same track. Jones was bound for Canton, Mississippi; he was behind schedule and was speeding to make up time. These are the facts, as told by Jones's fireman, Sim Webb; don't be surprised if this ballad departs from them.

CASEY JONES

Come all you rounders if you want to hear
The story of a brave engineer;
Casey Jones was the hogger's name,
On a big eight-wheeler, boys, he won his fame.
Caller called Casey at half-past four,
He kissed his wife at the station door,
Mounted to the cabin with orders in his hand,
And took his farewell trip to the promised land.

    Casey Jones, he mounted to the cabin,
    Casey Jones, with his orders in his hand!
    Casey Jones, he mounted to the cabin,
    Took his farewell trip into the promised land.

"Put in your water and shovel in your coal,
Put your head out the window, watch the drivers roll,
I'll run her till she leaves the rail,
'Cause we're eight hours late with the Western Mail!"
He looked at his watch and his watch was slow,
Looked at the water and the water was low,
Turned to his fireboy and said,
"We'll get to 'Frisco, but we'll all be dead!"

Casey Jones, he mounted to the cabin,
Casey Jones, with his orders in his hand!
Casey Jones, he mounted to the cabin,
Took his farewell trip into the promised land.

Casey pulled up Reno Hill,
Tooted for the crossing with an awful shrill,
Snakes all knew by the engine's moans
That the hogger at the throttle was Casey Jones.
He pulled up short two miles from the place,
Number Four stared him right in the face,
Turned to his fireboy, said, "You'd better jump,
'Cause there's two locomotives that's going to bump."

Casey Jones, he mounted to the cabin,
Casey Jones, with his orders in his hand!
Casey Jones, he mounted to the cabin,
Took his farewell trip into the promised land.

ANONYMOUS

This ballad is based on the true story of a Mississippi steamboat engineer — Jim Bludso, of Pike County, Illinois — who was burned to death while saving his passengers from a fire. The beauty and speed of the Mississippi riverboats led to great rivalries between their crews, and steamboat races — which sometimes resulted in fires from overworked furnaces — were not uncommon.

JIM BLUDSO

Wall, no! I can't tell whar he lives,
    Bekase he don't live, you see;
Leastways, he's got out of the habit
    Of livin' like you an' me.
Whar have you been for the last three year
    That you haven't heard folks tell
How Jimmy Bludso passed in his checks
    The night of the Prairie Belle?

He weren't no saint — them engineers
    Is pretty much all alike —
One wife in Natchez-under-the-Hill
    And another one here in Pike;
A keerless man in his talk was Jim,
    And an awkward hand in a row,
But he never flunked, an' he never lied —
    I reckon he never knowed how.

And this was all the religion he had —
    To treat his engine well;
Never be passed on the river;
    To mind the pilot's bell;

And if ever the Prairie Belle took fire,
  A thousand times he swore
He'd hold her nozzle agin the bank
  Till the last soul got ashore.

All the boats has their day on the Mississip',
  And her day come at last —
The Movastar was a better boat,
  But the Belle she wouldn't be passed.
And so she came tearin' along that night —
  The oldest craft on the line —
With a fellow squat on her safety-valve,
  And her furnace crammed, rosin an' pine.

The fire bust out as she cl'ared the bar
  And burnt a hole in the night,
And quick as a flash she turned, an' made
  For that willer-bank on the right.
There was runnin' an' cursin', but Jim yelled out
  Over all the infernal roar,
"I'll hold her nozzle agin the bank
  Till the last galoot's ashore!"

Through the hot black breath of the burnin' boat
  Jim Bludso's voice was heard,
An' they all had trust in his cussedness,
  And knowed he would keep his word.
And, sure's you're born, they all got off
  Afore the smokestack fell —
And Bludso's ghost went up alone
  In the smoke of the Prairie Belle.

He weren't no saint — but at Jedgement
    I'd run my chance with Jim,
'Longside of some pious gentlemen
    That wouldn't shook hands with him.
He seen his duty, a dead-sure thing —
    And went for it, thar an' then:
And Christ ain't a-goin' to be too hard
    On a man that died for men.

JOHN HAY

JOHN GILPIN

John Gilpin was a citizen
   Of credit and renown,
A train-band captain eke was he
   Of famous London Town.

John Gilpin's spouse said to her dear,
   "Though wedded we have been
These twice ten tedious years, yet we
   No holiday have seen.

"Tomorrow is our wedding-day
   And we will then repair
Unto the Bell at Edmonton,
   All in a chaise and pair.

"My sister and my sister's child,
   Myself, and children three,
Will fill the chaise; so you must ride
   On horseback after we."

He soon replied, "I do admire
   Of womankind but one,
And you are she, my dearest dear,
   Therefore it shall be done.

"I am a linen-draper bold,
   As all the world doth know,
And my good friend, the Calender,
   Will lend his horse to go."

Quoth Mrs. Gilpin, "That's well said;
  And for that wine is dear,
We will be furnish'd with our own,
  Which is both bright and clear."

John Gilpin kiss'd his loving wife;
  O'erjoy'd was he to find
That, though on pleasure she was bent,
  She had a frugal mind.

The morning came, the chaise was brought,
  But yet was not allowed
To drive up to the door, lest all
  Should say that she was proud.

So three doors off the chaise was stay'd,
  Where they did all get in,
Six precious souls, all agog
  To dash through thick and thin.

Smack went the whip, round went the wheels,
  Were never folk so glad;
The stones did rattle underneath,
  As if Cheapside were mad.

John Gilpin, at his horse's side,
  Seiz'd fast the flowing mane,
And up he got, in haste to ride,
  But soon came down again;

For saddle-tree scarce reach'd had he,
   His journey to begin,
When, turning round his head, he saw
   Three customers come in.

So down he came; for loss of time,
   Although it grieved him sore,
Yet loss of pence, full well he knew,
   Would trouble him much more.

'Twas long before the customers
   Were suited to their mind,
When, Betty, screaming, came downstairs,
   "The wine is left behind!"

"Good lack!" quoth he, "yet bring it me,
   My leathern belt likewise,
In which I bear my trusty sword
   When I do exercise."

Now mistress Gilpin (careful soul!)
   Had two stone-bottles found,
To hold the liquor that she loved,
   And keep it safe and sound.

Each bottle had a curling ear,
   Through which the belt he drew,
And hung a bottle on each side,
   To make his balance true.

Then over all, that he might be
    Equipp'd from top to toe,
His long red cloak, well brush'd and neat,
    He manfully did throw.

Now see him mounted once again
    Upon his nimble steed,
Full slowly pacing o'er the stones,
    With caution and good heed.

But finding soon a smoother road
    Beneath his well-shod feet,
The snorting beast began to trot,
    Which gall'd him in his seat.

So, "Fair and softly," John he cried,
    But John he cried in vain;
That trot became a gallop soon,
    In spite of curb and rein.

So stooping down, as needs he must
    Who cannot sit upright,
He grasp'd the mane with both his hands
    And eke, with all his might.

His horse, who never in that sort
    Had handled been before,
What thing upon his back had got
    Did wonder more and more.

Away went Gilpin, neck or nought;
    Away went hat and wig;
He little dreamt, when he set out,
    Of running such a rig.

The wind did blow, the cloak did fly,
    Like streamer long and gay,
Till loop and button failing both,
    At last it flew away.

Then might all people well discern
    The bottles he had slung;
A bottle swinging at each side,
    As hath been said or sung.

The dogs did bark, the children scream'd,
    Up flew the windows all;
And every soul cried out, Well done!
    As loud as he could bawl.

Away went Gilpin — who but he?
    His fame soon spread around,
"He carries weight! he rides a race!
    'Tis for a thousand pound!"

And still as fast as he drew near,
    'Twas wonderful to view
How in a trice the turnpike men
    Their gates wide open threw.

And now, as he went bowing down
   His reeking head full low,
The bottles twain behind his back
   Were shatter'd at a blow.

Down ran the wine into the road,
   Most piteous to be seen,
Which made his horse's flanks to smoke
   As they had basted been.

But still he seem'd to carry weight,
   With leathern girdle braced;
For all might see the bottle necks
   Still dangling at his waist.

Thus all through merry Islington
   These gambols he did play,
Until he came unto the Wash
   Of Edmonton so gay;

And there he threw the Wash about
   On both sides of the way,
Just like unto a trundling mop,
   Or a wild goose at play.

At Edmonton his loving wife
   From the balcony spied
Her tender husband, wondering much
   To see how he did ride.

"Stop, stop, John Gilpin! — Here's the house" —
   They all aloud did cry;
"The dinner waits, and we are tired."
   Said Gilpin, "So am I!"

But yet his horse was not a whit
   Inclin'd to tarry there;
For why? his owner had a house
   Full ten miles off, at Ware.

So like an arrow swift he flew,
   Shot by an archer strong;
So did he fly — which brings me to
   The middle of my song.

Away went Gilpin, out of breath,
   And sore against his will,
Till, at his friend the Calender's,
   His horse at last stood still.

The Calender, amazed to see
   His neighbor in such trim,
Laid down his pipe, flew to the gate,
   And thus accosted him.

"What news? what news? your tidings tell,
   Tell me you must and shall —
Say why bare-headed you are come,
   Or why you come at all?"

Now Gilpin had a pleasant wit,
    And loved a timely joke;
And thus, unto the Calender,
    In merry guise he spoke:

"I came because your horse would come,
    And, if I well forebode,
My hat and wig will soon be here,
    They are upon the road."

The Calender, right glad to find
    His friend in merry pin,
Return'd him not a single word,
    But to the house went in;

Whence straight he came, with hat and wig,
    A wig that flowed behind;
A hat not much the worse for wear,
    Each comely in its kind.

He held them up, and in his turn
    Thus show'd his ready wit:
"My head is twice as big as yours,
    They therefore needs must fit.

"But let me scrape the dust away,
    That hangs upon your face;
And stop and eat, for well you may
    Be in a hungry case."

Said John, "It is my wedding-day,
 And all the world would stare,
If wife should dine at Edmonton,
 And I should dine at Ware."

So, turning to his horse, he said,
 "I am in haste to dine;
'Twas for your pleasure you came here,
 You shall go back for mine."

Ah, luckless speech, and bootless boast!
 For which he paid full dear;
For, while he spake, a braying ass
 Did sing most loud and clear;

Whereat his horse did snort, as he
 Had heard a lion roar,
And gallop'd off with all his might,
 As he had done before.

Away went Gilpin, and away
 Went Gilpin's hat and wig;
He lost them sooner than at first,
 For why? — they were too big.

Now Mrs. Gilpin, when she saw
 Her husband posting down
Into the country far away,
 She pull'd out half-a-crown;

And thus unto the youth she said,
    That drove them to the Bell,
"This shall be yours, when you bring back
    My husband safe and well."

The youth did ride, and soon did meet
    John coming back again;
Whom in a trice he tried to stop,
    By catching at his rein;

But not performing what he meant,
    And gladly would have done,
The frightened steed he frighted more,
    And made him faster run.

Away went Gilpin, and away
    Went postboy at his heels,
The postboy's horse right glad to miss
    The rumbling of the wheels.

Six gentlemen upon the road
    Thus seeing Gilpin fly,
With postboy scampering in the rear,
    They rais'd a hue and cry:

"Stop thief! — stop thief! — a highwayman!"
    Not one of them was mute;
And all and each that passed that way
    Did join in the pursuit.

And now the turnpike gates again
  Flew open in short space:
The toll-men thinking as before
  That Gilpin rode a race.

And so he did, and won it too,
  For he got first to town;
Nor stopp'd till where he had got up
  He did again get down.

Now let us sing, long live the king,
  And Gilpin, long live he;
And, when he next doth ride abroad,
  May I be there to see.

WILLIAM COWPER

SKIPPER IRESON'S RIDE

Of all the rides since the birth of time,
Told in story or sung in rhyme —
On Apuleius's Golden Ass,
Or one-eyed Calender's horse of brass,
Witch astride of a human back,
Islam's prophet on Al-Borak —
The strangest ride that ever was sped
Was Ireson's, out of Marblehead!
    Old Floyd Ireson, for his hard heart,
    Tarred and feathered and carried in a cart
      By the women of Marblehead!

Body of turkey, head of owl,
Wings a-droop like a rained-on fowl,
Feathered and ruffled in every part,
Skipper Ireson stood in the cart.
Scores of women, old and young,
Strong of muscle, and glib of tongue,
Pushed and pulled up the rocky lane,
Shouting and singing the shrill refrain:
    "Here's Flud Oirson, fur his horrd horrt,
    Torr'd an' futherr'd an' corr'd in a corrt
      By the women o' Morble'ead!"

Wrinkled scolds with hands on hips,
Girls in bloom of cheek and lips,
Wild-eyed, free-limbed, such as chase
Bacchus round some antique vase,
Brief of skirt, with ankles bare,
Loose of kerchief and loose of hair,
With conch-shells blowing and fish-horns' twang,
Over and over the Maenads sang:

"Here's Flud Oirson, fur his horrd horrt,
Torr'd an' futherr'd an' corr'd in a corrt
    By the women o' Morble'ead!"

Small pity for him! — He sailed away
From a leaking ship in Chaleur Bay —
Sailed away from a sinking wreck,
With his own town's-people on her deck!
"Lay by! Lay by!" they called to him.
Back he answered, "Sink or swim!
Brag of your catch of fish again!"
And off he sailed through the fog and rain!
    Old Floyd Ireson, for his hard heart,
    Tarred and feathered and carried in a cart
        By the women of Marblehead!

Fathoms deep in dark Chaleur
That wreck shall lie forevermore.
Mother and sister, wife and maid,
Looked from the rocks of Marblehead
Over the moaning and rainy sea —
Looked for the coming that might not be!
What did the winds and the sea-birds say
Of the cruel captain who sailed away?
    Old Floyd Ireson, for his hard heart,
    Tarred and feathered and carried in a cart
        By the women of Marblehead!

Through the street, on either side,
Up flew windows, doors swung wide;
Sharp-tongued spinsters, old wives gray,
Treble lent the fish-horn's bray
Sea-worm grandsires, cripple-bound,
Hulks of old sailors run aground,

Shook head, and fist, and hat, and cane,
And cracked with curses the hoarse refrain:
  "Here's Flud Oirson, fur his horrd horrt,
  Torr'd an' furtherr'd an' corr'd in a corrt
    By the women o' Morble'ead!"

Sweetly along the Salem road
Bloom of orchard and lilac showed.
Little the wicked skipper knew
Of the fields so green and the sky so blue.
Riding there in his sorry trim,
Like an Indian idol glum and grim,
Scarcely he seemed the sound to hear
Of voices shouting, far and near:
  "Here's Flud Oirson, fur his horrd horrt,
  Torr'd an' futherr'd an' corr'd in a corrt
    By the women o' Morble'ead!"

"Hear me, neighbors!" at last he cried —
"What to me is this noisy ride?
What is the shame that clothes the skin
To the nameless horror that lives within?
Waking or sleeping, I see a wreck,
And hear a cry from a reeling deck!
Hate me and curse me — I only dread
The hand of God and the face of the dead!"
  Said old Floyd Ireson, for his hard heart,
  Tarred and feathered and carried in a cart
    By the women of Marblehead!

Then the wife of the skipper lost at sea
Said, "God has touched him! why should we!"
Said an old wife mourning her only son,
"Cut the rogue's tether and let him run!"

So with soft relentings and rude excuse,
Half scorn, half pity, they cut him loose,
And gave him a cloak to hide him in,
And left him alone with his shame and sin.
      Poor Floyd Ireson, for his hard heart,
      Tarred and feathered and carried in a cart
      By the women of Marblehead!

JOHN GREENLEAF WHITTIER

Around 1870 the longest railroad tunnel of the time, the Big Bend Tunnel, was being carved through the mountains of West Virginia. Men worked in pairs to break through the stubborn rock: the shaker held the six-foot steel drill while the driver struck blow after blow with a 10-pound hammer. The most powerful of the drivers was a six-foot-tall, 200-pound black man named John Henry. When the railroad company brought one of those newfangled steam drills to the Big Bend, John Henry vowed he would beat it.

JOHN HENRY

John Henry was a little baby,
   Setting on his mammy's knee,
Said, "The Big Bend Tunnel on the C. & O. Road
   Is gonna be the death of me,
     Lawd, gonna be the death of me."

One day his captain told him,
   How he had bet a man
That John Henry could beat his steam drill down,
   'Cause John Henry was the best in the land,
     John Henry was the best in the land.

John Henry kissed his hammer;
   White man turned on the steam;
Shaker held John Henry's steel;
   Was the biggest race the world had ever seen,
     Lawd, biggest race the world ever seen.

John Henry on the right side
   The steam drill on the left,
"Before I'll let your steam drill beat me down,
   I'll hammer my fool self to death,
     Hammer my fool self to death."

Captain heard a mighty rumbling,
    Said, "The mountain must be caving in."
John Henry said to the captain,
    "It's my hammer sucking de wind,
        My hammer sucking de wind."

John Henry said to his captain,
    "A man ain't nothin' but a man,
But before I'll let dat steam drill beat me down,
    I'll die wid my hammer in my hand,
        Lawd, die wid my hammer in my hand."

John Henry hammering on the mountain,
    The whistle blew for half-past two,
The last words his captain heard him say,
    "I've done hammered my insides in two,
        Lawd, I've hammered my insides in two."

The hammer that John Henry swung
    It weighed over twenty pound;
He broke a rib in his left-hand side,
    And John Henry fell on the ground.
        Lawd, John Henry fell on the ground.

They took John Henry to the river,
    And buried him in the sand,
And every locomotive come a-roaring by,
    Says, "There lies that steel-drivin' man,
        Lawd, there lies that steel-drivin' man!"

ANONYMOUS

GROUP 4
BALLADS
OLD

AND

NEW

THE BALLAD OF THE OYSTERMAN

It was a tall young oysterman lived by the river-side,
His shop was just upon the bank, his boat was on the tide;
The daughter of a fisherman, that was so straight and slim,
Lived over on the other bank, right opposite to him.

It was the pensive oysterman that saw a lovely maid,
Upon a moonlight evening, a-sitting in the shade;
He saw her wave her handkerchief, as much as if to say,
"I'm wide awake, young oysterman, and all the folks
    away."

Then up arose the oysterman, and to himself said he,
"I guess I'll leave the skiff at home, for fear that folks should
    see;
I read it in the story-book, that, for to kiss his dear,
Leander swam the Hellespont — and I will swim this
    here."

And he has leaped into the waves, and crossed the shining
    stream,
And he has clambered up the bank, all in the moonlight
    gleam;
Oh, there were kisses sweet as dew, and words as soft as
    rain —
But they have heard her father's step, and in he leaps again!

Out spoke the ancient fisherman, "Oh, what was that, my
    daughter?"
" 'Twas nothing but a pebble, sir, I threw into the water."

"And what is that, pray tell me, love, that paddles off so
    fast?"
"It's nothing but a porpoise, sir, that's been a-swimming
    past."

Out spoke the ancient fisherman, "Now bring me my
    harpoon!
I'll get into my fishing-boat, and fix the fellow soon."
Down fell that pretty innocent, as falls a snow-white lamb,
Her hair drooped round her pallid cheeks, like seaweed on
    a clam.

Alas for those two loving ones! she waked not from her
    swound,
And he was taken with the cramp, and in the waves was
    drowned;
But Fate has metamorphosed them, in pity of their woe,
And now they keep an oyster-shop for mermaids down
    below.

OLIVER WENDELL HOLMES

ODE TO BILLY JOE

It was the third of June, another sleepy, dusty, delta day;
I was out choppin' cotton, and my brother was bailin' hay;
And at dinner time we stopped and walked back to the
    house to eat,
And Mama hollered at the back door, "Y'all remember to
    wipe your feet."
Then she said, "I got some news this mornin' from
    Choctaw Ridge;
Today Billy Joe McAllister jumped off the Tallahatchie
    Bridge."

Papa said to Mama, as he passed around the black-eyed
    peas,
"Well, Billy Joe never had a lick o' sense, pass the biscuits
    please;
There's five more acres in the lower forty I've got to plow,"
And Mama said it was a shame about Billy Joe anyhow.
Seems like nothin' ever comes to no good up on Choctaw
    Ridge,
And now Billy Joe McAllister's jumped off the Tallahatchie
    Bridge.

Brother said he recollected when he and Tom and Billy Joe
Put a frog down my back at the Carroll County picture
    show,
And wasn't I talkin' to him after church last Sunday night?
"I'll have another piece of apple pie — you know, it don't
    seem right.
I saw him at the sawmill yesterday on Choctaw Ridge,
And now you tell me Billy Joe's jumped off the Tallahatchie
    Bridge."

Mama said to me, "Child, what's happened to your
    appetite?
I been cookin' all mornin' and you haven't touched a single
    bite;
That nice young preacher Brother Taylor dropped by today;
Said he'd be pleased to have dinner on Sunday — Oh, by
    the way,
He said he saw a girl that looked a lot like you up on
    Choctaw Ridge,
And she and Billy Joe was throwin' somethin' off the
    Tallahatchie Bridge."

A year has come and gone since we heard the news 'bout
    Billy Joe;
Brother married Becky Thompson, they bought a store in
    Tupelo;
There was a virus goin' round, Papa caught it and he died
    last spring,
And now Mama doesn't seem to want to do much of
    anything.
And me I spend a lot of time pickin' flowers up on
    Choctaw Ridge,
And drop them into the muddy water off the Tallahatchie
    Bridge.

BOBBIE GENTRY

In the northern part of England, near the Scottish border, there lived in medieval times several wealthy and powerful families who considered themselves neither English nor Scottish — and who refused to be governed by either side. The Armstrongs were such a family, although the Johnnie Armstrong of this ballad may be fictitious.

JOHNNIE ARMSTRONG

There dwelt a man in fair Westmoreland,
    Johnnie Armstrong men did him call;
He had neither land nor rents coming in,
    Yet he kept eight score men in his hall.

He had horse and harness for them all,
    Fine steeds all milky white;
The golden bands about their necks,
    And their weapons, were all alike.

News was then brought unto the king,
    That there was such a one as he,
That he lived free as a bold outlaw
    And robbed all the north country.

The king he wrote a letter then,
    He wrote it large and long;
He signed it with his royal hand
    And promised to do him no wrong.

When this letter came to Johnnie,
    His heart was blithe as birds on the tree.
"Never was an Armstrong sent for by the king;
    Not my father, my grandfather, nor none but me.

"And if we go before the king,
    We must go right orderly;
Each man of you shall have his scarlet coat,
    Laced with silver laces three.

"Each one shall have his velvet coat,
    Laced with silver lace so white,
With the golden bands about your necks,
    Black hats and white feathers alike."

By the morrow morning at ten of the clock
    To Edinburgh gone was he;
And with him all of his eight score men —
    A goodly sight for to see!

When Johnnie came before the king
    He sank down on his knee;
"Oh, pardon, my sovereign liege," he cried.
    "Pardon my eight score men and me."

"Thou shalt have no pardon, thou traitor bold,
    Not thy eight score men nor thee;
Tomorrow morning at ten of the clock
    Thou shalt all hang on the gallows tree."

Johnnie looked over his left shoulder,
    And a grievous look looked he;
Saying, "Asking grace of a graceless face —
    Why there is none for you nor me."

But Johnnie had a bright sword by his side,
    That he drew forth and swung so free,
That had the king not quickly stepped aside,
    He'd have smitten his head from his fair body.

Saying, "Fight on, fight on, my merry men,
    And see that none of you be ta'en;
For rather than men shall say we were hanged,
    Let them say how we were slain."

Then the men of fair Edinburgh rose,
    And so beset poor Johnnie 'round,
That fourscore and ten of Johnnie's best men
    Lay gasping all upon the ground.

Then like a madman Johnnie laid about,
    Like a madman then fought he,
Until a coward Scot came at Johnnie behind
    And ran him through his fair body.

Johnnie cried, "Fight on, my merry men all,
    And see that none of you be ta'en.
I'll lie down to bleed for a while,
    Then I'll rise and fight again."

News then was brought to young Johnnie Armstrong,
    As he stood by his nurse's knee,
And he vowed that if he lived to be a man,
    On the treacherous Scots revenged he'd be.

ANONYMOUS

LORD RANDALL

"Where have you been all the day, Randall, my son?
Where have you been all the day, my pretty one?"
"I've been to my sweetheart's, Mother;
Oh, make my bed soon,
For I'm sick to my heart and I fain would lie down."

"What did she feed you, Randall, my son?
What did she feed you, my pretty one?"
"Eels boiled in broth, Mother;
Oh, make my bed soon,
For I'm sick to my heart and I fain would lie down."

"Oh, I fear you are poisoned, Randall, my son,
I fear you are poisoned, my pretty one."
"Oh, yes, I am poisoned, Mother;
Make my bed soon,
For I'm sick to my heart and I fain would lie down."

"What will you leave your mother, Randall, my son?
What will you leave your mother, my pretty one?"
"A dead son to bury, Mother;
Oh, make my bed soon,
For I'm sick to my heart and I fain would lie down."

"What will you leave your sweetheart, Randall, my son?
What will you leave your sweetheart, my pretty one?"
"A rope to hang her, Mother;
Oh, make my bed soon,
For I'm sick to my heart and I fain would lie down."

ANONYMOUS

MAY COLVIN

False Sir John a-wooing came,
    To a maid of beauty rare;
May Colvin was the lady's name,
    Her father's only heir.

He wooed her indoors, he wooed her out,
    He wooed her night and day;
Until he got the lady's consent,
    To mount and ride away.

"Go fetch me some of your father's gold
    And some of your mother's fee,
And I'll carry you to the far Northland
    And there I'll marry thee."

She's gone to her father's coffers,
    Where all his money lay;
And she's taken the red, and she's left the white,
    And lightly she's tripped away.

She's gone down to her father's stable,
    Where all his steeds did stand;
And she's taken the best and left the worst,
    That was in her father's land.

He rode on, and she rode on,
    They rode a long summer's day,
Until they came to a broad river,
    An arm of a lonesome sea.

"Leap off the steed," says false Sir John;
    "Your bridal bed you see;
For it's seven fair maids I have drownèd here,
    And the eighth one you shall be.

"Cast off, cast off your silks so fine,
    And lay them on a stone,
For they are too fine and costly
    To rot in the salt sea foam."

"Oh, turn about, thou false Sir John,
    And look to the leaf o' the tree;
For it never became a gentleman
    A naked woman to see."

He's turned himself straight round about
    To look to the leaf o' the tree;
She's twined her arms about his waist,
    And thrown him into the sea.

"Oh, hold a grip of me, May Colvin,
    For fear that I should drown;
I'll take you home to your father's gates,
    And safe I'll set you down."

"Oh, safe enough I am, Sir John,
    And safer I will be;
For seven fair maids have you drownèd here,
    The eighth shall not be me.

"Oh, lie you there, thou false Sir John,
    Oh, lie you there," said she,
"For you lie not in a colder bed
    Than the one you intended for me."

So she went on her father's steed,
    As swift as she could away;
And she came home to her father's gates
    At the breaking of the day.

Up then spake the pretty parrot:
    "May Colvin, where have you been?
What has become of false Sir John,
    That wooed you yestere'en?"

"Oh, hold your tongue, my pretty parrot,
    Nor tell no tales on me;
Your cage will be made of the beaten gold
    With spokes of ivory."

Up then spake her father dear,
    In the chamber where he lay:
"What ails you, pretty parrot,
    That you prattle so long ere day?"

"There came a cat to my door, master,
    I thought 'twould have worried me;
And I was calling on May Colvin
    To take the cat from me."

ANONYMOUS

The poet and prophet Thomas of Erceldowne, who lived in England in the 12th or 13th century, was famous for his truthfulness. Two or three hundred years after his death, this ballad was composed about him and his supposed encounter with a fairy queen.

TRUE THOMAS

True Thomas lay on Huntlie bank;
    A marvel he did see;
For there he saw a lady bright
    Come riding down by the Eildon tree.

Her skirt was of the grass-green silk
    Her cloak of the velvet fine;
On every lock of her horse's mane
    Hung fifty silver bells and nine.

True Thomas he pulled off his cap,
    And bowed low down on his knee;
"All hail, thou mighty Queen of Heaven!
    For thy peer on earth could never be."

"Oh, no; oh, no, Thomas," she said,
    "That name does not belong to me;
I'm but the Queen of Fair Elfland,
    That hither am come to visit thee.

"Walk and talk, Thomas," she said,
    "Walk and talk along with me;
And if ye dare to kiss my lips,
    Sure of your body I will be!"

"If it be good, or if it be bad,
    That fate shall never frighten me."

Then he has kissed her on the lips,
    All underneath the Eildon tree.

"Now ye must go with me," she said,
    "True Thomas, ye must go with me;
And ye must serve me seven years,
    Through weal or woe, as may chance to be."

She's mounted on her milk-white steed,
    She's taken True Thomas up behind;
And aye, when'er her bridle rang,
    The steed flew swifter than the wind.

Oh, they rode on, and farther on,
    The steed flew swifter than the wind;
Until they reached a desert wide,
    And living land was left behind.

"Light down, light down now, Thomas," she said,
    "And lean your head upon my knee;
Light down, and rest a little space,
    And I will show you marvels three.

"Oh, see ye not yon narrow road,
    So thick beset with thorns and briers?
That is the path of righteousness,
    Though after it but few enquires.

"And see ye not yon broad, broad road,
    That stretches far and wide and even?
That is the path of wickedness,
    Though some may call it the road to heaven.

"And see ye not yon bonny road,
　　That winds about the green hillside?
That is the way to fair Elfland,
　　Where you and I this night must bide.

"But, Thomas, ye shall hold your tongue,
　　Whatever ye may hear or see;
For if ye speak word in Elfinland,
　　Ye'll ne'er win back to your own countree!"

Oh, they rode on, and farther on;
　　They waded through rivers above the knee,
And they saw neither sun nor moon,
　　But they heard the roaring of a sea.

It was dark, dark night; there was no starlight;
　　They waded through red blood to the knee;
For all the blood that's shed on earth,
　　Runs through the springs o' that countree.

At last they came to a garden green,
　　And she pulled an apple from on high —
"Take this for thy wages, True Thomas;
　　It will give thee the tongue that can never lie!"

"My tongue is my own," True Thomas he said,
　　"A goodly gift ye would give to me!
I never could hope to buy or sell
　　At fair or tryst where I may be.

"I never could speak to prince or peer,
   Nor ask of grace from fair lady."
"Now hold thy peace!" the lady said,
   "For as I say, so must it be."

He has gotten a coat of the even cloth,
   And a pair of shoes of the velvet green;
And till seven years were gone and past,
   True Thomas on earth was never seen.

ANONYMOUS

GROUP 5

LOVE

AND

LOYALTY

LOCHINVAR

Oh, young Lochinvar is come out of the West,
Through all the wide Border his steed was the best,
And save his good broadsword he weapons had none,
He rode all unarm'd and he rode all alone.
So faithful in love, and so dauntless in war,
There never was knight like the young Lochinvar.

He stay'd not for brake, and he stopp'd not for stone,
He swam the Eske river where ford there was none,
But ere he alighted at Netherby gate,
The bride had consented, the gallant came late;
For a laggard in love and a dastard in war
Was to wed the fair Ellen of brave Lochinvar.

So boldly he enter'd the Netherby hall,
'Mong bridesmen and kinsmen and brothers and all.
Then spoke the bride's father, his hand on his sword
(For the poor craven bridegroom said never a word),
"Oh, come ye in peace here, or come ye in war,
Or to dance at our bridal, young Lord Lochinvar?"

"I long woo'd your daughter, my suit you denied;
Love swells like the Solway, but ebbs like its tide;
And now I am come, with this lost love of mine
To lead but one measure, drink one cup of wine.
There are maidens in Scotland more lovely, by far,
That would gladly be bride to the young Lochinvar."

The bride kissed the goblet, the knight took it up,
He quaff'd off the wine and he threw down the cup.
She look'd down to blush, and she look'd up to sigh,
With a smile on her lips and a tear in her eye.

He took her soft hand ere her mother could bar:
"Now tread we a measure," said young Lochinvar.

So stately his form, and so lovely her face,
That never a hall such a galliard did grace,
While her mother did fret, and her father did fume,
And the bridegroom stood dangling his bonnet and plume,
And the bridesmaidens whisper'd, "'Twere better by far
To have match'd our fair cousin with young Lochinvar."

One touch to her hand, and one word in her ear,
When they reach'd the hall-door, and the charger stood
    near;
So light to the croup the fair lady he swung,
So light to the saddle before her he sprung!
"She is won! we are gone, over bank, bush, and scaur;
They'll have fleet steeds that follow," quoth young
    Lochinvar.

There was mounting 'mong Graemes of the Netherby clan;
Forsters, Fenwicks, and Musgraves, they rode and they ran;
There was racing and chasing on Cannobie Lee,
But the lost bride of Netherby ne'er did they see.
So daring in love, and so dauntless in war,
Have ye e'er heard of gallant like young Lochinvar?

SIR WALTER SCOTT

The erl-king, or king of the elves, was a wicked goblin who haunted the Black Forest of Germany and tried to lure children to their destruction. This poem about one of his appearances was set to music by Franz Schubert in 1816, and became one of the composer's best-known songs.

THE ERL-KING

Who rides so late in a night so wild?
A father is riding with his child.
He clasps the boy close in his arm;
He holds him tightly, he keeps him warm.

"My son, you are trembling. What do you fear?"
"Look, father, the Erl-King! He's coming near!
With his crown and his shroud! Yes, that is he!"
"My son, it's only the mist you see."

"O lovely child, oh, come with me,
Such games we'll play! So glad we'll be!
Such flowers to pick! Such sights to behold!
My mother will make you clothes of gold!"

"O father, my father, did you not hear
The Erl-King whispering in my ear?"
"Lie still, my child, lie quietly.
It's only the wind in the leaves of the tree."

"Dear boy, if you will come away,
My daughters will wait on you every day;
They'll give you the prettiest presents to keep;
They'll dance when you wake and they'll sing you asleep."

"My father! My father! do you not see
The Erl-King's pale daughters waiting for me?"
"My son, my son, I see what you say —
The willow is waving its branches of gray."

"I love you — so come without fear or remorse.
And if you're not willing, I'll take you by force!"
"My father! My father! Tighten your hold!
The Erl-King has caught me — his fingers are cold!"

The father shudders. He spurs on his steed.
He carries the child with desperate speed.
He reaches the courtyard, and looks down with dread.
There in his arms the boy lies dead.

JOHANN WOLFGANG VON GOETHE

TRANSLATED BY LOUIS UNTERMEYER

MAUD MULLER

Maud Muller, on a summer's day,
Raked the meadow sweet with hay.

Beneath her torn hat glowed the wealth
Of simple beauty and rustic health.

Singing, she wrought, and her merry glee
The mock-bird echoed from his tree.

But when she glanced to the far-off town,
White from its hill-slope looking down,

The sweet song died, and a vague unrest
And a nameless longing filled her breast —

A wish that she hardly dared to own,
For something better than she had known.

The Judge rode slowly down the lane,
Smoothing his horse's chestnut mane.

He drew his bridle in the shade
Of the apple-trees, to greet the maid,

And asked a draught from the spring that flowed
Through the meadow across the road.

She stooped where the cool spring bubbled up,
And filled for him her small tin cup,

And blushed as she gave it, looking down
On her feet so bare, and her tattered gown.

"Thanks!" said the Judge; "a sweeter draught
From a fairer hand was never quaffed."

He spoke of the grass and flowers and trees,
Of the singing birds and the humming bees;

Then talked of the haying and wondered whether
The cloud in the west would bring foul weather.

And Maud forgot her brier-torn gown,
And her graceful ankles bare and brown;

And listened, while a pleased surprise
Looked from her long-lashed hazel eyes.

At last, like one who for delay
Seeks a vain excuse, he rode away.

Maud Muller looked and sighed: "Ah me!
That I the Judge's bride might be!

"He would dress me up in silks so fine,
And praise and toast me at his wine.

"My father should wear a broadcloth coat;
My brother should sail a painted boat.

"I'd dress my mother so grand and gay,
And the baby should have a new toy each day.

"And I'd feed the hungry and clothe the poor,
And all should bless me who left our door."

The Judge looked back as he climbed the hill,
And saw Maud Muller standing still.

"A form more fair, a face more sweet,
Ne'er hath it been my lot to meet.

"And her modest answer and graceful air
Show her wise and good as she is fair.

"Would she were mine, and I today,
Like her, a harvester of hay;

"No doubtful balance of rights and wrongs,
Nor weary lawyers with endless tongues,

"But low of cattle and song of birds,
And health and quiet and loving words."

But he thought of his sisters, proud and cold,
And his mother, vain of her rank and gold,

So, closing his heart, the Judge rode on,
And Maud was left in the field alone.

But the lawyers smiled that afternoon,
When he hummed in court an old love-tune;

And the young girl mused beside the well
Till the rain on the unraked clover fell.

He wedded a wife of richest dower,
Who lived for fashion, as he for power.

Yet oft, in his marble hearth's bright glow,
He watched a picture come and go;

And sweet Maud Muller's hazel eyes
Looked out in their innocent surprise.

Oft, when the wine in his glass was red,
He longed for the wayside well instead;

And closed his eyes on his garnished rooms
To dream of meadows and clover-blooms.

And the proud man sighed, with a secret pain,
"Ah, that I were free again!

"Free as when I rode that day,
Where the barefoot maiden raked her hay."

She wedded a man unlearned and poor,
And many children played round her door.

But care and sorrow, and childbirth pain,
Left their traces on heart and brain.

And oft, when the summer sun shone hot
On the new-mown hay in the meadow lot,

And she heard the little spring brook fall
Over the roadside, through the wall,

In the shade of the apple-tree again
She saw a rider draw his rein;

And, gazing down with timid grace,
She felt his pleased eyes read her face.

Sometimes her narrow kitchen walls
Stretched away into stately halls;

The weary wheel to a spinet turned,
The tallow candle an astral burned,

And for him who sat by the chimney lug,
Dozing and grumbling o'er pipe and mug,

A manly form at her side she saw,
And joy was duty and love was law.

Then she took up her burden of life again,
Saying only, "It might have been."

Alas for maiden, alas for Judge,
For rich repiner and household drudge!

God pity them both! and pity us all,
Who vainly the dreams of youth recall.

For of all sad words of tongue or pen,
The saddest are these: "It might have been!"

Ah, well! for us all some sweet hope lies
Deeply buried from human eyes;

And, in the hereafter, angels may
Roll the stone from its grave away!

JOHN GREENLEAF WHITTIER

During the Civil War the Southern cavalry — soldiers on horseback — stormed around the countryside raiding public property, seizing horses, burning bridges, and capturing railroad supplies. In 1863 General John Hunt Morgan and his men, known as "Morgan's Raiders," swept through Tuscawaras County, Ohio, with the Michigan cavalry close on their heels.

KENTUCKY BELLE

Summer of 'sixty-three, sir, and Conrad was gone away —
Gone to the county town, sir, to sell our first load of hay.
We lived in the log house yonder, poor as ever you've seen;
Roschen there was a baby, and I was only nineteen.

Conrad, he took the oxen, but he left Kentucky Belle;
How much we thought of Kentuck, I couldn't begin to
    tell —
Came from the Bluegrass country; my father gave her to me
When I rode north with Conrad, away from Tennessee.

Conrad lived in Ohio — a German he is, you know —
The house stood in broad cornfields, stretching on, row
    after row;
The old folks made me welcome; they were kind as kind
    could be;
But I kept longing, longing, for the hills of the Tennessee.

Oh, for a sight of water, the shadowed slope of a hill!
Clouds that hang on the summit, a wind that never is still!
But the level land went stretching away to meet the sky —
Never a rise, from north to south, to rest the weary eye!

From east to west, no river to shine out under the moon,
Nothing to make a shadow in the yellow afternoon;
Only the breathless sunshine, as I looked out, all forlorn,
Only the "rustle, rustle," as I walked among the corn.

When I fell sick with pining we didn't wait any more,
But moved away from the cornlands out to this river
    shore —
The Tuscarawas it's called, sir — off there's a hill, you
    see —
And now I've grown to like it next best to the Tennessee.

I was at work that morning. Someone came riding like mad
Over the bridge and up the road — Farmer Rouf's little lad.
Bareback he rode; he had no hat; he hardly stopped to say,
"Morgan's men are coming, Frau, they're galloping on this
    way.

"I'm sent to warn the neighbors. He isn't a mile behind;
He sweeps up all the horses — every horse that he can
    find;
Morgan, Morgan the raider, and Morgan's terrible men,
With bowie knives and pistols, are galloping up the glen."

The lad rode down the valley, and I stood still at the
    door —
The baby laughed and prattled, playing with spools on the
    floor;
Kentuck was out in the pasture; Conrad, my man, was
    gone;
Near, near Morgan's men were galloping, galloping on!

Sudden I picked up baby and ran to the pasture bar:
"Kentuck!" I called; "Kentucky!" She knew me ever so far!
I led her down the gully that turns off there to the right,
And tied her to the bushes; her head was just out of sight.

As I ran back to the log house at once there came a
    sound —

The ring of hoofs, galloping hoofs, trembling over the
     ground,
Coming into the turnpike out from the White-Woman
     Glen —
Morgan, Morgan the raider, and Morgan's terrible men.

As near they drew and nearer, my heart beat fast in alarm;
But still I stood in the doorway, with baby on my arm.
They came; they passed; with spur and whip in haste they
     sped along;
Morgan, Morgan the raider, and his band six hundred
     strong.

Weary they looked and jaded, riding through night and
     through day;
Pushing on east to the river, many long miles away,
To the border strip where Virginia runs up into the west,
And for the Upper Ohio before they could stop to rest.

On like the wind they hurried, and Morgan rode in
     advance;
Bright were his eyes like live coals, as he gave me a side-
     ways glance;
And I was just breathing freely, after my choking pain,
When the last one of the troopers suddenly drew his rein.

Frightened I was to death, sir; I scarce dared to look in his
     face,
As he asked for a drink of water and glanced around the
     place;
I gave him a cup, and he smiled — 'twas only a boy, you
     see,
Faint and worn, with his blue eyes; and he'd sailed on the
     Tennessee.

Only sixteen he was, sir — a fond mother's only son —
Off and away with Morgan before his life had begun!
The damp drops stood on his temples; drawn was the boy-
　　ish mouth;
And I thought me of the mother waiting down in the
　　South!

Oh, plucky was he to the backbone and clear grit through
　　and through;
Boasted and bragged like a trooper; but the big words
　　wouldn't do;
The boy was dying, sir, dying, as plain as plain could be,
Worn out by his ride with Morgan up from the Tennessee.

But, when I told the laddie that I too was from the South,
Water came in his dim eyes and quivers around his mouth.
"Do you know the Bluegrass country?" he wistful began to
　　say,
Then swayed like a willow sapling and fainted dead away.

I had him into the log house, and worked and brought him
　　to;
I fed him and coaxed him, as I thought his mother'd do;
And, when the lad got better, and the noise in his head was
　　gone,
Morgan's men were miles away, galloping, galloping on!

"Oh, I must go," he muttered; "I must be up and away!
Morgan, Morgan is waiting for me! Oh, what will Morgan
　　say?"
But I heard a sound of tramping and kept him back from
　　the door —
The ringing sound of horses' hoofs that I had heard before.

And on, on came the soldiers — the Michigan cavalry —
And fast they rode, and black they looked galloping
    rapidly;
They had followed hard on Morgan's track; they had fol-
    lowed day and night;
But of Morgan and Morgan's raiders they had never caught
    a sight.

And rich Ohio sat startled through all those summer days,
For strange, wild men were galloping over her broad
    highways;
Now here, now there, now seen, now gone, now north,
    now east, now west,
Through river valleys and corn-land farms, sweeping away
    her best.

A bold ride and a long ride! But they were taken at last.
They almost reached the river by galloping hard and fast;
But the boys in blue were upon them ere ever they gained
    the ford,
And Morgan, Morgan the raider, laid down his terrible
    sword.

Well, I kept the boy till evening — kept him against his
    will —
But he was too weak to follow, and sat there pale and still;
When it was cool and dusky — you'll wonder to hear me
    tell —
But I stole down to that gully and brought up Kentucky
    Belle.

I kissed the star on her forehead — my pretty, gentle
    lass —
But I knew that she'd be happy back in the old Bluegrass;

A suit of clothes of Conrad's, with all the money I had,
And Kentuck, pretty Kentuck, I gave to the worn-out lad.

I guided him to the southward as well as I knew how;
The boy rode off with many thanks, and many a backward
    bow;
And then the glow it faded, and my heart began to swell,
As down the glen away she went, my lost Kentucky Belle!

When Conrad came in the evening the moon was shining
    high;
Baby and I were both crying — I couldn't tell him why —
But a battered suit of rebel gray was hanging on the wall,
And a thin old horse with drooping head stood in Ken-
    tucky's stall.

Well, he was kind, and never once said a hard word to me;
He knew I couldn't help it — 'twas all for the Tennessee;
But, after the war was over, just think what came to pass —
A letter, sir; and the two were safe back in the old
    Bluegrass.

The lad had got across the border, riding Kentucky Belle;
And Kentuck she was thriving, and fat, and hearty, and
    well;
He cared for her, and kept her, nor touched her with whip
    or spur:
Ah! we've had many horses, but never a horse like her!

CONSTANCE FENIMORE WOOLSON

The Civil War brought suffering and grief to families all over the country. Each family lived in dread of the day a letter would come telling them of the grievous wounding or death of a beloved father, husband, or son.

COME UP FROM THE FIELDS FATHER

Come up from the fields father, here's a letter from our Pete
And come to the front door mother, here's a letter from thy
    dear son.

Lo, 'tis autumn,
Lo, where the trees, deeper green, yellower and redder,
Cool and sweeten Ohio's villages with leaves fluttering in
    the moderate wind,
Where apples ripe in the orchards hang and grapes on the
    trellis'd vines,
(Smell you the smell of the grapes on the vines?
Smell you the buckwheat where the bees were lately
    buzzing?)
Above all, lo, the sky so calm, so transparent after the rain
    and with wondrous clouds,
Below too, all calm, all vital and beautiful, and the farm
    prospers well.

Down in the fields all prospers well,
But now from the fields come father, come at the daughter's
    call,
And come to the entry mother, to the front door come right
    away,
Fast as she can she hurries, something ominous, her steps
    trembling,
She does not tarry to smooth her hair nor adjust her cap.

Open the envelope quickly,
Oh this is not our son's writing, yet his name is sign'd,
Oh a strange hand writes for our dear son, Oh stricken
    mother's soul!

All swims before her eyes, flashes with black, she catches
    the main words only,
Sentences broken, *gunshot wound in the breast, cavalry skir-*
    mish, taken to hospital,
At present low, but will soon be better.

Ah now the single figure to me,
Amid all teeming and wealthy Ohio with all its cities and
    farms,
Sickly white in the face and dull in the head, very faint,
By the jamb of a door leans.

Grieve not so, dear mother (the just-grown daughter speaks
    through her sobs,
The little sisters huddle around speechless and dismay'd),
See, dearest mother, the letter says Pete will soon be better.

Alas poor boy, he will never be better (nor may-be needs to
    be better, that brave and simple soul),
While they stand at home at the door he is dead already,
The only son is dead.

But the mother needs to be better,
She with thin form presently drest in black,
By day her meals untouch'd, then at night fitfully sleeping,
    often waking,
In the midnight waking, weeping, longing with one deep
    longing,

Oh that she might withdraw unnoticed, silent from life
    escape and withdraw,
To follow, to seek, to be with her dear dead son.

WALT WHITMAN

THE GOLDEN GLOVE

A wealthy young squire of Tamworth we hear,
He courted a nobleman's daughter so fair;
To marry this lady it was his intent,
All friends and relations gave gladly consent.

The time was appointed for their wedding day,
A young farmer chosen to give her away;
As soon as the farmer this lady did spy,
He inflamed her heart; "Oh my heart!" she did cry.

She turned from the squire, but nothing she said;
Instead of being married she took to her bed.
The thought of the farmer ran sore in her mind;
A way to secure him she quickly did find.

Coat, waistcoat, and breeches she then did put on,
And a-hunting she went with her dog and her gun;
She hunted around where the farmer did dwell,
Because in her heart she did love him full well.

She oftentimes fired, but nothing she killed,
At length the young farmer came into the field;
And as to discourse with him was her intent,
With her dog and her gun to meet him she went.

"I thought you had been at the wedding," she cried.
"To wait on the squire, and give him his bride."
"No, sir," said the farmer, "if the truth I may tell,
I'll not give her away, for I love her too well."

"Suppose that the lady should grant you her love?
You know that the squire your rival would prove."

"Why, then," says the farmer, "with sword-blade in hand,
By honor I'll gain her when she shall command."

It pleased the lady to find him so bold;
She gave him a glove that was flowered with gold,
And she told him she found it when coming along,
As she was a-hunting with dog and with gun.

The lady went home with a heart full of love,
And she gave out a notice that she'd lost a glove;
And said, "Who has found it, and brings it to me,
Whoever he is, he my husband shall be."

The farmer was pleased when he heard of the news,
With heart full of joy to the lady he goes.
"Dear honored lady, I've picked up your glove,
And hope you'll be pleased to grant me your love."

"It already is granted, and I'll be your bride;
I love the sweet breath of a farmer," she cried.
"I'll be mistress of dairy, and milking the cow,
While my jolly brisk farmer sings sweet at the plow."

And when she was married she told of her fun,
And how she went a-hunting with dog and with gun.
"And now I have got him so fast in my snare,
I'll enjoy him forever, I vow and declare."

ANONYMOUS

LADY CLARE

It was the time when lilies blow,
    And clouds are highest up in air,
Lord Ronald brought a lily-white doe
    To give his cousin, Lady Clare.

I trow they did not part in scorn:
    Lovers long-betrothed were they:
They two will wed the morrow morn —
    God's blessing on the day!

"He does not love me for my birth,
    Nor for my lands so broad and fair;
He loves me for my own true worth,
    And that is well," said Lady Clare.

In there came old Alice the nurse,
    Said, "Who was this that went from thee?"
"It was my cousin," said Lady Clare,
    "Tomorrow he weds with me."

"Oh, God be thanked!" said Alice the nurse,
    "That all comes round so just and fair:
Lord Ronald is heir of all your lands,
    And you are *not* the Lady Clare."

"Are ye out of your mind, my nurse, my nurse,"
    Said Lady Clare, "that ye speak so wild?"
"As God's above," said Alice the nurse,
    "I speak the truth: you are my child.

"The old earl's daughter died at my breast;
    I speak the truth, as I live by bread!

I buried her like my own sweet child,
    And put my child in her stead."

"Falsely, falsely have ye done,
    O mother," she said, "if this be true,
To keep the best man under the sun
    So many years from his due."

"Nay now, my child," said Alice the nurse,
    "But keep the secret for your life,
And all you have will be Lord Ronald's,
    When you are man and wife."

"If I'm a beggar born," she said,
    "I will speak out, for I dare not lie.
Pull off, pull off, the brooch of gold,
    And fling the diamond necklace by."

"Nay now, my child," said Alice the nurse,
    "But keep the secret all you can."
She said, "Not so: but I will know
    If there be any faith in man."

"Nay now, what faith?" said Alice the nurse,
    "The man will cleave unto his right."
"And he shall have it," the lady replied,
    "Though I should die tonight."

"Yet give one kiss to your mother dear.
    Alas, my child, I sinned for thee."
"O mother, mother, mother," she said,
    "So strange it seems to me.

"Yet here's a kiss for my mother dear,
    My mother dear, if this be so,
And lay your hand upon my head,
    And bless me, mother, ere I go."

She clad herself in a russet gown,
    She was no longer Lady Clare:
She went by dale, and she went by down,
    With a single rose in her hair.

The lily-white doe Lord Ronald had brought
    Leaped up from where she lay,
Dropped her head in the maiden's hand,
    And followed her all the way.

Down stepped Lord Ronald from his tower:
    "O Lady Clare, you shame your worth!
Why come you dressed like a village maid,
    That are the flower of the earth?"

"If I come dressed like a village maid,
    I am but as my fortunes are:
I am a beggar born," she said,
    "And not the Lady Clare."

"Play me no tricks," said Lord Ronald,
    "For I am yours in word and in deed.
Play me no tricks," said Lord Ronald,
    "Your riddle is hard to read."

Oh, and proudly stood she up!
    Her heart within her did not fail;
She looked into Lord Ronald's eyes,
    And told him all her nurse's tale.

He laughed a laugh of merry scorn:
    He turned and kissed her where she stood.
"If you are not the heiress born,
    And I," said he, "the next in blood —

"If you are not the heiress born,
    And I," said he, "the lawful heir,
We two will wed tomorrow morn,
    And you shall still be Lady Clare."

ALFRED, LORD TENNYSON